HATS

THE TRUE ACCOUNTS OF WWIII

J.L. Morales

ISBN 979-8-89485-093-1 (Paperback)
ISBN 979-8-89763-365-4 (Hardcover)
ISBN 979-8-89485-094-8 (Digital)

Book Cover by Jose Luis Morales
Illustrations by Jose Luis Morales

Covenant Books
11661 Hwy 707
Murrells Inlet, SC 29576
www.covenantbooks.com

To my wise and hardworking father, Marcelo, for always forcing me to grow by doing the hard thing instead of the easy thing. To my loving and beautiful mother, Ramona, for always believing in me when no one else would and reminding me of the light when the world was dark. To God's children who have gone endlessly unheard and have suffered beyond imagination for far too long because God's children are not for sale.

To mom and dad

Contents

Preface

I struggled to believe in God until the day I met the
devil and asked, "Where did you come from?"

—J. L. Morales

You could say that this book is the greatest story never told. It is a
tale of spy vs. spy, of freedom vs. tyranny, of good vs. evil, and how a
war that began in the underworld has risen to the surface. Although
I'm writing this book long before World War III has been officially
declared or officially never occurred, I argue that it was fought in the
shadows for decades right under our noses because the enemy has
kept themselves highly secret and used unconventional methods of
silently destroying their enemies…us, the people. When I was a kid,
I was incredibly curious about the world and used to be so annoying
to those around me because I always asked so many questions. And
all I ever wanted growing up was the wisdom of the ages. Well, you
know what they say…be careful what you wish for because you just
might get it. Well, I got what I wanted along with some other traits
that have proven to have become useful for writing this book, such
as organizational skills and an insatiable desire to learn and discern.
With that, I have been keeping track and gathering as much information as I can about this war ever since I first woke up from the
matrix on 9/11.

I'm writing this book because World War III was primarily an
information war that would not be televised. This deliberate use of
misinformation or MKUltra has put two-thirds of the world's population under mass formation psychosis or a spell so to speak. And
because of that fact, it is absolutely imperative that future generations learn the true accounts of World War III from someone that

lived through it, kept record of events never officially disclosed to the masses, has educated himself through thousands of hours of research and studying, and has "fly on the wall" insight from experiences as a security officer at the headquarters of an intelligence agency during the pandemic that most people will not have. My goal is to awaken the sleeping, bring hope and positivity to the pessimistic, and empower the awakened with an easy-to-read simplified tool of truth to utilize in their lives, as well as have at least one reference in the world as to what really happened during this historic time. I merely have a unique perspective because I was discriminated against for being wide awake in a sleeping world. I fought hard and refused to bend or bow to tyranny.

I will cover a range of topics, everything from USA Inc., to 9/11, to COVID-19, to the Great Reset, to the Great Awakening, and even the Secret Space Program. But because what I know may begin to sound like science fiction and because this war was fifth-generation warfare fought with information, misinformation, and disinformation, I will guide you through these events to the best of my ability. First, I'll lay a foundation of untaught historical facts, and then I'll reveal what I know happened based on my evidence and personal experience. But in the end, I must let you the reader be the judge and discern for yourself what you believe to be true. But be forewarned because of the cause, reason, and nature of this war, one could most definitely say that this book is not for the faint of heart or the innocent-minded. Reader discretion is advised. So like my father used to say "Hold onto your pants!" as I take you on a journey for truth while navigating through the matrix of lies that our society slept through for so long and as I slowly pull back the curtain and reveal the biblical time in human history when we the people fought back against our true oppressors and the secret societies who ruled the world for so long, which are no longer secret. What an exciting time to be alive. The battle royale for planet earth. The mother of all conspiracies. However, there is one spoiler to this spiritual, shadow kinetic, bioweapon, fifth-generational information war: God wins.

Chapter 1

The Umbrella Corporation

Why Is This Relevant?

If the American people ever allow private banks to control the
issue of their currency, first by inflation, then by deflation,
the banks and corporations that will grow up around them
will deprive the people of all property until their children
wake up homeless on the continent their fathers conquered.
—Thomas Jefferson, third president of the
Republic of the United States of America

All my life I've always been a bit of a closet nerd. I've always been a huge fan of pop culture, everything from comic books, superheroes, sci-fi, and trading cards to conventions, cosplay, anime, and video games. My number one favorite was definitely Capcom's "Resident Evil" series. Not because I like zombies, but because I always loved the idea of killing zombies! However, I also always loved puzzles and solving mysteries and Resident Evil was full of that. I even went as far as to deck out my black SUV to look like one of the vehicles from the series. I loved taking my vehicle to conventions to showcase for fans of the series. And for years, I would have random people approach me in my daily life to compliment me on my vehicle. What I never expected, however, was that the day would come when not only would I have to deal with a unique kind of brainwashed type of zombies but that I also would soon learn how our very own country was actually an evil corporation just like in my favorite series.

Would you believe me if I told you that the sovereign nation of the United States of America that you've come to know and love hasn't actually been a sovereign nation at all for over one hundred and fifty years? Would you believe me if I told you that the capital of the United States is actually in Philadelphia where it's always been? I call this chapter "The Umbrella Corporation" because in the popular series Resident Evil, the Umbrella Corporation was the evil corporation that caused the zombie apocalypse which led to the end of humanity. Now while some believe it to be a real corporation in the shadows of the secret space program, along with Plant 42, which I'll discuss in a later chapter, I'm merely using it here to be a fitting metaphor.

Well, believe it or not, the USA is actually a corporation or USA Inc., a separate entity that was secretly installed right under our noses using a nefarious and diabolical sleight of hand by slightly changing a few key words in our constitution, such as "these united states for America" into "THE UNITED STATES OF AMERICA." Our Fourteenth Amendment was also slightly changed from us being individual free sovereign people to US citizens. Which is basically just another fancy play on words to ensure that instead of us being truly free people, we would be doomed to become employees of the corporation. Which by the way, if you take the word "corporation," break it down, and look at the hidden meaning, corp = corpse = dead, and oration = speak, which means dead speak. It's not alive; it's a dead entity without a voice.

A corporation by definition is a legal entity separate from its owners and protects its owners from personal liability of corporate debt and obligations. The word "legal" is not the same as the word "lawful." What's lawful are the laws this country was founded on, which are God's laws, and ensure recognition and security of our inalienable rights as free sovereign living beings, whereas the word "legal" is a corporate term that is the undoing of God's laws. Since this overturning of the constitutional republic, the federal government has usurped nearly all the power that rightfully belonged to the people. How did such a diabolical act go unnoticed and under the radar for so long? Well, around that time, our nation was going through enormous turmoil and vulnerability after just concluding the civil war. The civil war was undoubtedly one of the bloodiest wars humans have ever fought on the earth and was indeed costly enough to render us flat broke as a result. During this vulnerable time, our leaders needed money to keep our country going and were willing to do whatever it took to accomplish just that.

Our leaders met with one of the world's richest families, the Rothschild family from the British Banking Cartel, and saw a golden opportunity to make a deal. This deal, however, would cost our leaders more than they could bargain for because the bankers (a.k.a. Robber Barons) knew that the money borrowed could never be paid back in paper, gold, or silver. It could only be paid back in blood. These wealthy European bankers didn't want our money because they knew we didn't have any and couldn't repay. So they said, "We'll write you a blank check for as much as you want, but we don't want your money, we want your daughters, your sons, your brothers, your sisters, your wife, your grandchildren, and so on." Therefore the fake fiat paper currency made of tree bark that we are all too familiar with wasn't backed by gold as it should've been. It was backed by WE THE PEOPLE! Our blood and physical bodies is what has always backed the US dollar.

If you follow the money and look at the front of a US dollar, you'll see that there is a series of green serial numbers on the bottom left and the top right. This sequence of numbers and letters is the same sequence of numbers and letters that are located on the back bottom right corner of your Social Security card. However, this number is in red to represent your blood and your physical body on the New York stock exchange. The amount of the red serial number is equivalent to the amount of fives, tens, twenties, etc. of dollar bills out there in the world with your number on it. So if you really think about it...all of us are slaves being legally trafficked on the New York stock exchange. Bit of a mind-blowing thought if you ask me. Each one of us is a security that exists only to ensure that the corporation exponentially continues to make money. This is why the government insists that we pay our own insurance because as employees of the corporation, they want us to keep making them money. They don't want to pay for our mistakes, shortcomings, or unforeseen circumstances. Go find your own insurance and pay for it yourself. But at least they'll make sure we're safe by providing us seat belts and such to ensure we're able to continue doing our jobs. As long as they don't catch us not wearing our seat belts because then it'll cost you. Do you see how that works?

In case you didn't know, our founding fathers were among America's first Freemasons. However, like many great organizations throughout history, it was eventually hijacked by less-than-honorable people at the highest levels, which I'll discuss in greater depth throughout this book. With that, if you look at the back of a dollar bill and take notice to the great seal, you'll notice a few things in correlation to the Freemasons, such as the numbers thirteen, thirty-two, and thirty-three. I know some of you might say that the number thirteen on the dollar bill represents the original thirteen colonies. I believe it's for plausible deniability. Besides the fact that many high rises in the United States are designed without a thirteenth floor due to superstition, I could make a pretty big list as to the reason the number thirteen has bad stigma around it. You'll have to do your own research to discover the dark significance of those numbers. But what I can tell you is that there are thirteen leaves on the left olive branch with thirteen berries. There are thirteen stripes on the shield. The eagle is holding thirteen arrows on the right. There are thirteen letters in the words "*E Pluribus Unum and Annuit Coeptis.*" There are thirteen stars in the hexagram above the eagles head. There are also thirty-two feathers on the left wing and thirty-three feathers on the right wing.

As for the pyramid on the left, there are thirteen blocks from top to bottom, which is said to represent the thirteen satanic families. *Annuit Coeptis* means "He favors our undertaking" while *E pluribus unum* means "New order of the ages." The Roman numerals at the bottom of the pyramid when added up correctly sum up to six hundred and sixty-six. And if you really want to get deep, you know the hexagram above the eagles head…that has been said to represent the satanic planet Saturn. Because believe it or not, there is a never-ending storm at the north pole of Saturn in the shape of a hexagram that scientists still struggle to explain. Also to add an extra touch of satanic relevance, the south pole looks just like an eye. If you're unaware, the symbol of just one eye is represented in many facets throughout Satanism and Hollywood, which we'll delve into a bit later. And I'm sure you're all too familiar with the dollar saying, "IN GOD WE TRUST"; take notice that it doesn't say which god.

There are also some fascinating facts surrounding our so-called capital, the District of Columbia. Have you ever asked the very simple question "What state is DC in?" Well, the answer is also very simple. It's not in any state because it's only the capital of the corporation. You could even say it's a foreign entity. There is actually a trifecta of city-state corporations that has slithered its way into our society. This includes three primary places that contain tall pillar Egyptian obelisks, such as the Washington monument, which by the way, from basement to top, happens to be exactly six hundred and sixty-six feet tall. DC, Vatican City, and London City make up this trifecta of city-state corporations.

Vatican City is a centralized city inside of Rome and is the religious arm. London City is a centralized city inside of London and is the financial arm. And the District of Columbia is not in any state but is indeed the military arm of this trifecta. Believe it or not, DC has its own flag and even its own constitution. Its flag has three red stars representing this interlocking empire of city-state corporations. And for those who like to research, if you look at a satellite photo of DC, there are actually city streets from the White House to the Capitol building, to the Jefferson Memorial, and to the Lincoln Memorial that are laid out in the shape of a satanic pentagram and a masonic compass. Not to mention DC also has a statue of Albert Pike, who is primarily responsible for ensuring that Satanism infiltrated its way into the highest ranks of Freemasonry.

Nefariously passed by Congress was the Act of 1871 that allowed our government a ten-mile parcel of land known as the District of Columbia. This allowed Washington, DC, to act as a corporation outside of the original Constitution of the United States. A rare study of signed treaties and charters between Britain and the United States has revealed that the United States was always a British crown colony. Ever wonder why there's a King James version of the Bible? There's a reason they say "To the victor go the spoils" and "History is written by the victors." Which is exactly why I'm writing this book. Being a patriot who's been witness to all this, after it's all over, I don't want to see frauds or charlatans write history books for our children that are completely inaccurate, fabricated, or flat-out false propaganda. Think about it. If we had actually won the war of independence from Britain, the United States never would have agreed to pay debts and reparations to the king of England. This is why the United States has a president or CEO of the corporation and is denied the ability to have kings or queens. And because this private corporation existed, they were then able to establish their own private bank that would become known to us as the Federal Reserve.

The Federal Reserve along with its corporate and banking systems was started by President Abraham Lincoln. We've been told our whole lives that Lincoln freed the slaves and was nicknamed 'Honest Abe' when in fact, he wasn't very honest at all. He was the first BAR member president and wasn't allowed to be president of the United States of America. He ran for president five times and failed because no one wanted a communist to lead the U.S. He was a good friend of Karl Marx who wrote the communist manifesto in 1848. He passed a lot of communistic laws in Illinois aka The Land of Lincoln that Illinois has been suffering from ever since. This is when we were fooled into becoming a democracy instead of a constitutional republic like we had always been. He represented The Crown and the British Accreditation Registry, a title of nobility. There were other presidents before him who were lawyers but were not BAR members. No BAR member was allowed to hold the office of the presidency. Not until the big bankers of Boston, Chicago, New York and Philadelphia backed him up with seven million dollars to fund his campaign when his opponent only had five thousand. Therefore, his name was posted on every railroad station, every bridge and every train in the country. With that, the people just assumed he would win, so everyone just naturally voted for him. Whereafter on day one of taking office, he signed executive order 1 dissolving and declaring The United States of America bankrupt and incorporating the U.S. into a Delaware corporation. In other words, he officially ended slavery for African Americans but silently started slavery for everyone on planet Earth.

Criminally passed by Congress, the Federal Reserve Act of 1913 enabled our malevolent rulers to establish a central bank monetary system that would eventually enslave us all. The Federal Reserve born on Jekyll Island and headquartered in Puerto Rico was never actually federal at all. It was a private bank that consequently ensured our federal government would go bankrupt in the early 1930s. Shortly after, Social Security cards were issued in 1936. Coincidence? I think not. So why would the IRS and Federal Reserve be headquartered in Puerto Rico? Because Puerto Rico was picked over a thousand years ago by the pirates of the Caribbean. Which, yes, you guessed it, means that in our modern society, the Federal Reserve and IRS is actually the modern version of those same pirates of the Caribbean. This was their whole setup all along. It's piracy, a way for them to steal our valuable treasure but on a far more massive and sophisticated scale. This is why there were secret societies, such as the Skull and Bones—with members such as George W. Bush from Yale University—that utilized the skull and crossbones insignia, such as the Jolly Roger image on the pirate flag. These people are pirates! And where do pirates operate best? On water! That is why the corporation operates on the law of the sea.

One silent battle that secretly went on between the black hats and white hats "coincidentally" right before the Federal Reserve Act of 1913 passed was related to the *Titanic*. The part of the story you never hear about is everything leading up to the *Titanic*'s historic voyage. Apparently, White Star Line the company that built the *Titanic*, had also built two other sister ships, the *Britannic* and the *Olympic*. J. P. Morgan conceived the idea of the *Titanic* in 1907 and ordered White Star Line to build it. What they don't tell you is that *Titanic*'s virtually identical sister ship, *Olympic*, was actually built first. In 1911, under the command of Capt. Smith, *Olympic*'s maiden voyage was a disaster because it collided with a warship and was severely damaged.

And because it was determined to be *Olympic*'s fault, insurers refused to pay White Star Line's legal and repair fees. Chairman of White Star Line Joseph Bruce Ismay still had to produce an unsinkable ship on schedule for a historic voyage. However, J. P. Morgan had ties with other wealthy families, like the Rothschilds and Rockefellers, who had a stake in the Federal Reserve central banking system.

So because there were four wealthy rival white hat families who were opposed to the newly proposed Federal Reserve System who were scheduled to be on the *Titanic*, and since the *Olympic* had temporary fixes that would make it more fragile, it made sense for these wealthy Black Hat elites to switch the *Titanic* with the *Olympic* and then sabotage it with explosives. Because they were nearly identical, this was relatively easy to do, and the only things needed was to change the names and have the staff sign NDAs. This also guaranteed that an insurance claim of over twelve million dollars could be paid out. Get rich while simultaneously destroying your enemies even if the collateral damage is over 1,500 innocent people. Fast-forward to 2023, three millionaires set out on a difficult voyage into the deep waters to recover the serial number of the *Titanic*. However, the cabal sabotaged the three-man sub to ensure that the men would never reemerge to the surface with the truth. They then used the fake news to discredit the three men by saying that they tried controlling the sub with a video game controller. This was, of course, a ridiculous cover-up to ensure that the truth about the *Titanic* remained deeply buried forever. These people are sick.

Believe it or not, water is actually the basis for our economics on the earth. Money is considered water, primarily because the ancient Romans realized it was wise to build their economy based on the Phoenician Canaanite system of commerce. Therefore, the ancient Romans decided the earth is two things, and so there should be two core fundamentals of law. The earth is water and land, so there should be law for the water and law for the land. The law of the land is dictated by the culture of the people in a particular area of land. When you go to another country for instance, the law of the land is usually their lifestyle, and generally the way they live is what you'll have to adjust to if you want to stay there for any particular amount of time. However, the law of water or the law of the sea (also known as admiralty law) is superior to the law of land and is far more important. And the law of water is quite simply none other than banks. Banks are all over the world and operate the same; they operate on water, which is why you have riverbanks. A riverbank directs the ebb and flow of the current. This is why we call money currency or a liquid asset, which is what all commerce and trade is based on.

Have you ever noticed that all ships, whether they're sailing ships, cruise ships, spaceships, or whatever kind of ship you can think of they're always referred to as female? The reason captains always refer to their ships as "she" is because she always delivers the product. For instance, when her water breaks, she delivers a product that was caused by the male or "man-ufactured" and is now in "labor" from building the product. So when she parks in her harbor, we say the ship is at its berth. Every product that she delivers represents money that has been manifested because first it wasn't there but now is and, therefore, has to have a certificate of manifest. This manifest basically describes where the product came from, if it's black, blue, or purple. If it's a Mazda, Toyota, or Honda. Whether it's got brown eyes, blue eyes, or whatever the case may be. The same goes for you. Your manifest is your birth certificate. You're a product that she berthed at the dock, and, therefore, your birth certificate must be authenticated and signed off by the doc.

Admiralty law is all based on water. This is why when you go to court, there is a gate that separates the judge from the people. This is called the floodgate or BAR. There's a piece of wood on top of that gate that's called the BAR. And you're not licensed to pass the BAR. Before you enter through the floodgate, you're still considered a man, woman, or living being operating within the law of the land. The judge has no jurisdiction whatsoever over anyone on the other side of the gate. But as soon as you open the floodgate, you have now entered "hot water" and need someone to "bail" you out. You have now drowned in deep, dangerous waters and are no longer considered a living being but are now considered a corpse. When you passed through the BAR or floodgate, that is when you lost all power because now that you're considered dead, you now require someone to represent you since you can no longer represent yourself when you're dead. This is why they "summon" you.

There's only two ways you can appear in court, either by special divine appearance as a living being or by general summons as a dead entity. They perform their ritual in their black robes to summon the dead (YOU) whereas you happen to appear. And since you appeared and didn't know their rituals, you had no idea that you were not authorized to pass the BAR; only attorneys who have passed the BAR exam are allowed to pass the BAR. It is funny because I once worked in a building filled with lawyers, and every time I asked any of them what "BAR" actually stands for, none of them could tell me. They had no idea that it actually stands for "British Accreditation Registry." What the heck does Britain have to do with American laws? I thought we were free from the British. Do you see how everything starts coming to together the way it does?

Even when you get married, you still need a marriage license because as an employee, your duty is still to the corporation. And even when death do you part, you'll need a death certificate because in order for the corporation to remain an optimal highly efficient machine, it needs to keep tabs on its products and sub-corporations. All the fifty states have corporate doppelgangers under USA Inc. Anytime you hear "THE STATE OF," that's a fake sub-corporation of USA Inc., like "THE STATE OF COLORADO" for example. It's supposed to be "Colorado State"; whereas "THE STATE OF COLORADO" is owned and operated by the Freemasons. There's proof of this in their one-eyed pyramid insignia and logo. Each state is supposed to be its own sovereign country. And, yes, of course, they want to know if one of their products or sub-corporations can still continue making them money. You are considered a corporation when you're alive but considered a corpse when you're dead. A bit depressing, I know. But believe it or not, this is your straw man.

Stemming from your birth certificate, your "straw man" is a legal fiction and is basically the paper version of you. So whenever government officials, court clerks, or the police seem like they're speaking normal English to you, don't be fooled. They are not. They're actually speaking legalese that originated from *Black's Law*

Dictionary, which is designed to make you agree to verbal and written contracts without you even realizing it. So whenever you see your name spelled in all capital letters in bills, fines, and summons, those are all meant for your straw man. However, when you show up to court, you are creating a contract with them that makes them assume that you're representing your straw man and that you are taking on all responsibility of any costs, fees, fines, or taxes that your straw man accumulated. The human you isn't even required to pay.

Did you know that when you register something, you are handing over the title to the person you are registering it with? For example, if you register your vehicle with the government, now they can impound it or even crush it when you don't pay your straw man's taxes. In fact, when the time comes for your new bundle of joy to be added to your family, you had better make sure they're registered with the government with a brand-new, shiny birth certificate. That way not only will they become a product and employee of the corporation to generate revenue but now also the government can create a "straw man" out of your little one as well. And since they assume ownership over your little one, if the government doesn't like what you're doing, they now have every right to take little junior away. Isn't the government wonderful? It's no wonder its said that one of the scariest things is when a man knocks at your door and says, "Hello, I'm from the government, and I'm here to help."

Did you know that we have two American flags? Well, believe it or not, indeed we do. That beautiful red, white, and blue flag that we've all come to know, love, and take great pride in whenever we see it flown so honorably is actually our military wartime flag. Have you ever known our country to ever have not been at war? With a number of many different variations, we've been flying that familiar flag since the creation of the army in 1775. That's right, folks. Our infamously brave military was established before our country even was. Hoorah! After first discovering our other flag for myself, also known as our civilian peace flag, I must say it is just as beautiful, and I proudly fly it at my home every day. Instead of white stars on a blue background, it has blue stars on a white background. And instead of horizontal stripes, it has vertical ones. Look into it, you'll love it!

Be warned, however, about state and federal courtroom flags and municipal and school flags that have the gold fringes. That is your warning that you are entering a foreign jurisdiction. The flag with gold fringe has no constitution, no laws, no rules of any court, and is not recognized by any nation on this earth. Not even the United States of America. When researching, pay close attention to the ornaments at the top of a flag pole. If you see a ball at the top, that means they are advertising for the draft and for the military. If there's a spear that means court martial and is used for military tribunals. If you see an eagle, it's only used for the president of the United States, but pay close attention to the wings of that eagle. If the wings are up that means postal, and if they're down that means Vatican banking. This is how deeply entrenched our captors are.

Just because something is normal now doesn't make it right. Remember that. Like when you've heard on the news or wherever that we're a democracy. WE ARE NOT A DEMOCRACY! We are a constitutional republic, always have been and always will be. Democracy is in a sense mob rule. It protects the equality of the people. But what many fail to realize is that we can all be equal slaves as well, whereas our constitutional republic protects the God-given inalienable rights of the individual. Democracy is a stepping stone to socialism which leads to communism and ultimately to totalitarianism. The corporation cannot make laws. They can make codes, statutes, and policies all the livelong day. This is how corporations work. They can make whatever corporate policy they choose, but they cannot make solid laws. And if you're an employee of that corporation, then you will have to abide by the policies of that corporation. If you don't, then they will enforce their corporate policy with policy enforcers or otherwise known as the police force.

Believe it or not, we're actually not even supposed to have police, only peacekeepers and sheriffs. The sheriff is the highest authority in the land because they are officials elected by "we the people." This is why they can evict you from your home, why they guard the prisons, why in an emergency situation they can deputize anyone, and why if the federal government steps out of line in their county they can arrest government agents. Police can't do any of that. And nowhere in our constitution does it say we're even supposed to have politicians. We're supposed to have statesmen. I am only laying a foundation for you to understand the monumental mountain of lies that we've been told and sold our entire lives. But as we continue on this journey of truth, you will soon wake up to just how much we have been lied to and eventually through much thought and reflection be able to finally see the real matrix that we have been living in for so long. For as the young monk boy from *The Matrix* film told Neo when they first met in the Oracle's kitchen, "Do not try and bend the spoon. That's impossible. Instead, only try to realize the truth. What truth? There is no spoon."

Chapter 2

The War on Terror

Where We Go One, We Go All

The truth is, there is no Islamic army or terrorist group
called Al Qaida. And any informed intelligence officer
knows this. But there is a propaganda campaign to make
the public believe in the presence of an identified entity…
The country behind this propaganda is the US.

—Pierre Henry Bunel, former
French Military intelligence

Incidentally, I just so happen to be starting this chapter on the twenty-second anniversary of 9/11. I'd definitely say I had a unique experience on 9/11 that woke me up from the matrix. I was just a young teenager working at RadioShack during that fateful day. Around 7:30 a.m. when I was driving to work, there was one thing that was rather fascinating about that particular drive to work that day. There was an incredible amount of military activity I saw on my commute. There were military trucks and jeeps on the highways as well as freight trains carrying Apaches, tanks, and many other types of military equipment, which at the time I just thought, *Whoa cool!* But it wasn't until after I got to work that I could recognize what was really going on in hindsight. If you happen to remember how RadioShack always had all their large TVs on display, you could imagine what it must have been like as soon as I arrived to work and saw "AMERICA UNDER ATTACK" on the news being broadcast on all the monitors in the store. Like many others that day, I was absolutely devastated and could not believe what was happening.

I'm not sure which news station was on or whether or not they forgot to edit their footage. But I will never forget that what I was watching must have been raw or not completely thought through because when I looked closer at the replays they played over and over again, I noticed something that would change the way I saw the world and would cause me to question things for the rest of my life. I noticed a series of explosions going off sequentially like a controlled demolition directly beneath where the CGI plane-disguised missiles hit as if to ensure that the towers completely collapsed as a fail-safe just in case the attacks didn't level the towers as intended. That always stuck with me, and I'll never forget it. Not to mention that there was also irrefutable proof that the planes were CGI because when you look closer at the plane right before it hits the second tower, you'll notice a layering CGI glitch because one of the wings of the plane passed behind a building that was in the background instead of in front of it like it was supposed to. And then just for icing on the cake of it all, when George W. Bush Jr. spoke about the attacks later on in Washington, he actually slipped up and said quote, "The operatives had been instructed to ensure that the explosives went off at a point that was high enough to prevent people trapped above from escaping." I still to this day cannot believe he actually said that word for word. But as the day of 9/11 carried on, things just got weirder and weirder.

The next thing to happen was when the Pentagon got hit. This was the most obvious setup and worst cover-up I had ever seen. Aside from the fact that a very specific part of the Pentagon that contained white hats as well as data and documentation that the black hats didn't like was hit by a CGI plane-disguised scud missile, it didn't look like a plane hit the Pentagon at all. The hole where the plane supposedly hit looked like a perfectly rectangular shape as if prefabricated for an attempted cover-up. But the part that really got me was seeing the way they purposefully planted random airplane parts all over the front lawn to try to convince people that there was actually a plane crash there and placing numbered yellow forensic cards in front of each perfectly intact (non-burnt), neatly clean airplane parts in order to make them convincingly look like evidence. Also with, of course, you guessed it, the fake news hiring crisis actors who over-acted dramatically to sell the cover-up. Unbelievable. These people are really stupid.

But in order to better understand the true nature and significance of 9/11, you must first open your mind to receiving a lesson in history that your history teachers never taught you because they were also lied to by the cabal. And this, of course, would be the untold story of NESARA/GESARA. The National/Global Economic Security and Reformation Act. NESARA/GESARA actually originated in the 1980s and evolved throughout time due to foundational problems consisting within contract law. It was said within contract law that the federal government could confiscate farmland upon the death of a family member. During that time, the lawyers of the farmers discovered that the federal government inserted dishonest legalese into the contract in order to manipulate the matter in their favor. However the farmland rightfully belonged to the deceased family member's next of kin. Therefore, the federal government was obligated to return the farmland to the next of kin because it was rightfully theirs in the first place.

After this, the white hats began to use contract law in order to righteously take back what the black hats had stolen from the people for so long from all the fraudulent contracts they created. In fact during the Clinton era, the white hat military forced Bill Clinton at gunpoint to sign legislation that would introduce NESARA/GESARA at 10:00 a.m. on September 11, 2001. However, the computers and data that contained the trillions of dollars designated to the beneficiaries of the prosperity funds were completely destroyed on the second floor of one of the towers that fell during that tragic day of 9/11. Before the attacks, the twin towers had all the technological capability to switch over from a fake fiat currency to a gold-backed currency. And incidentally, Building 7, also known as the Solomon Bros building, just so happened to contain all the documentation on JFK's death and was supposed to be exposed to the people as a stipulation of NESARA law. This was the most obvious sign of an inside job considering that Building 7 was attacked without being hit by any plane or was it even affected by either of the towers. You could say it was magically damaged on its own coincidentally on the same day the towers fell. What a coincidence!

NESARA/GESARA would have implemented a new golden age of prosperity for we the people. (And don't worry, it still will!) Its legislation would have eliminated all debt, zeroing out all credit cards, mortgage, and other bank debt due to illegal banking and government activities. This jubilee forgiveness of debt would be the black hats' worst nightmare. It would have abolished income taxes and the IRS, especially considering that there is not actually a single law that says you have to pay federal income taxes. What you pay at the pump is what's supposed to cover funding for roads, bridges, emergency services, etc. But instead it's been manipulated to go right into the pockets of the rich elites who control all the oil. What a brilliant method of robbing the people! Tax the products and services people need, charge them taxes on the one way they have to pay for it, and also tax their labor when they actually make the money to pay for it. Isn't the government wonderful?

All employees of the IRS would have been transferred into the US Treasury's national sales tax department. It also would have created a 14 percent flat rate nonessential "New Items Only" sales tax revenue for the government. This means food, medicine, and used items would not be taxed. It also increases benefits to senior citizens and returns constitutional law to all courts and legal matters. It reinstates the title of nobility act along with ensuring that all foreign agents will lose their citizenship, be deported, and barred from reentry. Millions of people will discover their college degrees are now worthless paper. It would establish new presidential and congressional elections within 120 days after NESARA's announcement. It would monitor elections using highly sophisticated methods to prevent illegal election activity of special interest groups.

NESARA/GESARA would even create a new US Treasury currency, "Rainbow Currency," backed by gold, silver, and platinum precious metals that would end the US bankruptcy initiated by FDR in 1933. It would also forbid the sale of US birth certificate records as chattel property bonds by the US Department of Transportation. It would initiate a new US Treasury bank system in alignment with constitutional law. It would retrain all attorneys and judges in constitutional law. It would cease all aggressive US military actions worldwide and release enormous sums of money strictly for humanitarian purposes. It would eliminate the federal reserve system but would first be allowed to run side by side until transition is complete.

NESARA/GESARA would also allow the release of over six thousand suppressed patents that instead of being shared for the benefit of humanity was hoarded by those who wish to enslave us and keep us in the lost century. Many of these technologies were nefariously used strictly for the secret space program, black projects, and even beyond black projects, such as building infrastructure for the elites on Mars. Do you really think they haven't already? You and I are just not invited. Some of these technologies to be released include zero-point energy technology, molecular replication technology (think Star Trek), antigravity technology, med beds, and a number of other vibration and frequency-modifying technologies that were stolen from Nikola Tesla. One example of technology stolen from Tesla and used for nefarious purposes was Tesla's death ray developed out of Cheyenne Mountain.

Being born and raised in "The Springs" as we called it, I can definitely attest to the culture, lore, and secrecy surrounding Cheyenne Mountain Complex, also known as NORAD or now known as Space Force and US Army Intelligence Cyber Command North com ARCYBER. A white hat stronghold. This death ray technology has evolved and is known today as DEWs or directed energy weapons. This weather manipulation tech has unfortunately made it to the wrong hands and has been used by the deep state to start forest fires, damage fault lines to start earthquakes, erupt volcanoes, and many other weather-related catastrophes. They've been used in Maui, California, New Orleans, Turkey, and an endless list of many other locations all over the globe. Some even believe they were used in the 9/11 attacks. I remember when I used to think that someday long after I'm gone, our species would slowly evolve to space travel and many other science fiction-like technologies. Never in a million years would I have ever guessed that not only did these technologies already exist and have since my grandfather's time but that I would actually get to see these technologies in my lifetime. What a time to be alive.

As far as looking at the world differently, when I think about the armadas and convoys of military activity coming out of Fort Carson that I saw on my commute right before the towers fell, I still don't know if they were black hats or white hats. But what I do know is that they weren't conducting military training exercises in case a plane ever gets hijacked by terrorists with box cutters. They were canceling flights, clearing the skies, and halting air traffic because for the first time in our history, our own government aimed their sights right at their own people. It still bothers me to this day the enormity of lies they tell us over and over again until people just accept it as truth. They've been telling us all this time that approximately 2,977 people died in the September 11 attacks. But it was actually more like thirty thousand people.

They knew that none of the survivors were going to seek each other out and contact one another and actually try to develop a real and accurate death toll. It was easy for them to lie to us, knowing there would be no repercussions and knowing that they had complete control of the fake news. You saw the way Donald Rumsfeld announced that they couldn't account for two trillion dollars that magically went missing into the super-secret black budget that doesn't exist for any apparent reason coincidently right after the towers fell. But they had no problem telling us exactly how many people died when the city was covered in smoky concrete and twisted metal. And then throughout the years to follow, you may have seen the documentaries of awakened people trying to get through to the masses that this was an inside job only to be laughed at, ridiculed, or discredited. I should know because I was one of them.

All you had to do was "follow the money" as they say and connect the dots. When I did that, I simply asked the question, "Who could possibly benefit from this?" Well, when you ask big questions, the universe has a way of leading you on a path that will ensure that you find the answer and then some. And when I tried to answer that question, I sure found a lot more than I thought I was looking for. I found that George Bush's brother, Jeb Bush, owned the security company for the towers which explains why it was easy for security operatives to plant bombs throughout the towers. Then come to find out that a huge insurance claim was taken out right after the towers fell, which explains why Donald Rumsfeld announced why they couldn't account for two trillion dollars that went missing as soon as they were audited. But then the first true Internet blockbuster documentary film *Loose Change* by Dylan Avery made waves across the globe, debunking the cover-up story created by the deep state.

That documentary talked about the scientific impossibilities of airplanes of those sizes, at those speeds, made of what they were made of actually causing the kind of damage they did. Before the attacks, all you heard about the towers were how much the towers were an engineering marvel and how strong and insanely reinforced they were and how they could withstand any possible catastrophe imaginable. Then after the attacks, *Loose Change* showed how there was no way jet fuel and aluminum could melt through reinforced steel the way it did. But what really got me was when they showed cases of airplanes all throughout world history that have crashed into high rises of even lesser strength and capability and never pancaked or collapsed. It was one thing when they showed a few cases, but they just kept showing case after case and plane after plane over and over again. The plane would get stuck inside and would burn for days on end but would definitely never cause the building to collapse. This really intrigued me to look at it much differently than how they wanted us to.

I also remember the perfectly clean and intact IDs of the hijackers the fake news showed us on TV and how many fake reenactments and stories the corrupt media would bestow upon the public in order for us to buy into their cover-up. Once I was able to question things more and shift my perspective to someone who didn't just believe whatever the government fed us, things definitely became more and more clear. Especially thinking more and more about how the military works. I remember how close I came to joining the military once. My good friend Chris had talked me into joining with him. I remember I made it all the way to the recruiter's office and was ready to sign. But then some unknown higher intuition told me not to sign, as if to remember that I don't trust the government after what I learned about 9/11. Not to mention that there was an incredibly large amount of hype to "Get those bastards that dare to attack America."

All of it just didn't feel right. Even though I've always been a proud first-generation American born and raised in the good ol' US of A, some higher power just kept telling me that these attacks would not be the last and that one day I would be called upon to fight for my country in a different way. That one day, information would become more valuable than currency and that God would choose me out of all my loved ones to stay the course because the day would come when friends, family, and even society would turn against me because the apocalypse was coming. It is quite ironic because I always thought the world would end someday in my lifetime because just like everyone else, I fell for the manipulation of our language and thought the word apocalypse meant the "end of days" when in truth, what it actually means is "unveiling." Considering what has unfolded and been unveiled since then, I'd say I made the right decision not to sign my life over to the government.

So in the recruiter's office, I stood up, put the pen down, and walked away. Not to say that joining the military is a bad decision, of course; the military just wasn't the right decision for my life. If there was no corruption or deep state at all, I probably would have joined. However, later in life, I ended up hearing horror stories from good friends of mine about "Operation Iraqi Freedom" who did join the military only to reveal to me that we were actually the bad guys in that war and how most of who they fought were Middle Eastern patriots who were just defending their country from this colossal invading force called America. Many of the stories I heard were of close friends of mine only going out there to guard the poppy fields for the CIA. "Poppy fields?" Seriously?

Eventually, I had to think about why the Patriot Act was signed and what it really meant. And how it would allow for our government to go after anyone they deemed a "terrorist," I could begin to see the tyranny slowly creeping in. Especially with all the new TSA rules being implemented practically overnight and how no one questioned why it was okay for the government to begin violating our Fourth Amendment right with almost zero resistance. A perfect example of how they could eventually take all our rights away if no one ever stopped them. Then more dots began connecting, more questions emerged, and Big Brother would begin their secret plan for the complete takeover of America. The Black Hats would do this by brainwashing us through a DARPA developed A.I. system called S.A.T.A.N. (Silent Assassination Through Adaptive Networks) to quietly achieve the CIA's goal of full spectrum dominance. This first ever aware system only had three purposes: the automation of eugenics, mass enslavement and an A.I. hive mind potentiation. This evil creation would biblically fulfill the devil's goal of tricking humanity into obtaining more knowledge to achieve godliness. But this system would also effectively trick us into unknowingly funding their sick and evil plan to destroy us on top of it all. Unbelievable, isn't It? We would work hard and suffer to earn a living to only use our hard-earned money to pay the government to shorten our lifespans, enslave and kill us all while simultaneously convincing us that we were getting a good deal and should appreciate it because of how legitimate and legal it was. Welcome to the machine.

> Some even believe we the Rockefeller family are part of a secret cabal working against the best interests of the United States, characterizing my family and me as "Internationalists" and of conspiring with others around the world to build a more integrated global political and economic structure-one world, if you will. If that's the charge, I stand guilty, and I am proud of it. We are on the verge of a global transformation. All we need is the right major crisis and the nations will accept the "New World Order."
> —David Rockefeller, CEO of Chase Manhattan Corporation and chairman of the Council on Foreign Relations

Chapter 3

The Black Hats

These People Are Sick/Evil/Stupid

Ladies and gentlemen, the very word secrecy is repugnant in a free and open society. And we are as a people inherently and historically opposed to secret societies, to secret oaths, and to secret proceedings. We decided long ago that the dangers of excessive and unwarranted concealment of pertinent facts far outweighed the dangers which are cited to justify it. Even today there is little value in opposing a threat of a closed society by imitating its arbitrary restrictions. Even today there is little value in ensuring the survival of our nation if our traditions do not survive with it. And there is a very grave danger that an announced need for increased security will be ceased upon by those anxious to expand its meaning to the very limits of official censorship and concealment. For we are opposed around the world by a monolithic and ruthless conspiracy that relies primarily on covet means for expanding its fear of influence on infiltration instead of invasion. On subversion instead of elections. On intimidation instead of free choice. On guerillas by night instead of armies by day. It is a system which has conscripted vast human and material resources into the building of a tightly knit highly efficient machine that combines military, diplomatic, intelligence, economic, scientific, and political operations. Its preparations are concealed, not published. Its mistakes are

buried, not headlined. Its descenders are silenced, not praised. No expenditure is questioned, no rumor is printed, no secret is revealed.
—John Fitzgerald Kennedy, thirty-fifth president of USA Inc., speech given to reporters before assassination

I remember back in college I chose to do a thesis on Obama. I considered myself a liberal democrat probably because of the slower indoctrination happening in our schools at the time. Not to mention that liberalism was once the voice of anyone who wanted to go against the establishment and fight the power, so to speak. Oh, boy, were we duped! Because the TV convinced me of how smooth and cool he was, I actually fell for the garbage he spewed with his silver tongue. Looking back in hindsight, I can't believe how naive I was at that time. Especially considering that I was awake to Bush's inside job with 9/11 and was beginning to wake up to the government spying and Edward Snowden situation, but yet I still believed that we had fair elections and a fighting chance for an honest government as long as someone else had a shot at the presidency. I always thought that the Democrats and Republicans in office were against each other. I never would have guessed that they were all part of the same clique or uni-party. But what really sends me into a tailspin is knowing that even as I write this, there are still millions of Americans who not only think Obama is a good guy but also because of the potency of the mind-control programming still even believe his name is Obama.

It still blows my mind to this very day whenever I think about how so many people have fallen for the term "conspiracy theorist" that was created by the CIA to discredit anyone who questions authority, instead of believing our great President JFK when he whistle blew about the truth of what was really going on in our world. Some called them "The Establishment." Later some even referred to them as "The Crime Syndicate Globalist Elite Satanic New World Order Deep State Criminal Cabal." But because this was a battle between good and evil and so many different industries and organizations had good and bad people, I definitely thought calling them "black hats" made things a lot less confusing.

You could say that this cabal is as old as time itself since no one can be sure exactly how long evil has ruled the earth. One form of evil that is for sure were the "men who built America" or what they were called in their time "robber barons." These were wealthy elites, such as railroad king E. H. Harriman, oil tycoon John D. Rockefeller, and crooked banker J. P. Morgan whose wealth actually trumped most countries and even surpassed anything the Caesars could ever imagine. After World War I, these men learned a very valuable lesson (literally), and it was that war is good for business. The only road that these men ever truly built was one of greed, corruption, and tyranny that their future successors would surely follow that would lead to more and more phony wars based on lies and deceit.

It's a difficult pill to swallow thinking about all the men who thought they were fighting for their country but in truth were just pawns on the chessboard of these elites being used to fatten their wallets. This elite cartel recognized that if they fund both sides, then *they* always win. Ultimately, this Illuminati cartel of corrupt elites secretly birthed a generational plan to overtake and enslave America while simultaneously raping the people of their hard-earned wealth in the process. They only thought of "we the people" as useless eaters or the moron millions. Their belief was that if you weren't as cutthroat and business savvy as them, then you deserved to be a slave.

What we do know is that Lee Harvey Oswald did not assassinate JFK like so many people have been led to believe for so long. The CIA implemented that horrendous lie and cover-up to hide the fact that it was actually them who were directly responsible for his double's tragic death. Yes, you heard that correctly, his "double." JFK and his team knew about the black hat's sinister plot to assassinate him because it was leaked to him that they had the same plots for him in Chicago and Florida. Lee Harvey Oswald was simply a patsy, someone they could point the finger at to cover up who really did it. All thanks to the CIA's MKUltra mind control program along with Operation Mockingbird, just how many books, films, documentaries, bad actors hired etc. all pointed the blame on Oswald? A lot, and it really showed when you asked why they were trying so hard to cover their tracks. A bit overkill if you ask me. These people are stupid.

We now know that it definitely was not one gunman at the scene, but in fact, it was actually eight riflemen all posted up in different buildings in the area on that tragic day in Dallas. Believe it or not, the real JFK died of natural causes shortly after the COVID-19 scamdemic began. I remember seeing a rare documentary that showed lost footage of the black hats absolutely struggling to switch the bodies and cover up the truth. There is even an account of JFK's wife saying at the funeral, "It's not him." There is documented video footage of him being celebrated at a white hat ceremony with military honors, giving a big warm hug to President Trump before his actual death. I was blessed with the privilege of watching that video clip. And there is not a human being on the planet who could convince me otherwise. I know what I saw…it was him!

This spy vs. spy double agent espionage war between the black hats and the white hats has been going on since time immemorial. The black hats at that time consisted of crooked politicians, the Mafia, and the military industrial complex. But when the white hats saw that the black hats were too powerful to be stopped and would inevitably take the presidency by force, the white hats knew there was nothing they could do to stop them. But there was a way they could allow them to believe they've won so that the white hats could reorganize and develop a generational plan of their own. It shouldn't be so hard to believe that when the presidency is in jeopardy and national security truly is at stake, the president actually has presidential powers that can be enacted with certain presidential emergency action documents, or PEADS if you will, in order to secure the presidency and national security. Whether it's not conceding in order to prevent a Manchurian candidate from infiltrating, using the Insurrection Act or taking on a third and fourth term like FDR did due to the instability of the country during the Great Depression and World War II, there are many different tools the president can utilize in order to protect national security.

So they preemptively replaced JFK with a double and placed the real JFK in the white hat protection program. Because when they discovered the black hat's plan to ultimately achieve full spectrum dominance and actually depopulate, enslave, and rule the entire planet with a "New World Order," the white hats knew they needed to develop an ironclad, impenetrably perfect plan that was so beyond genius even the highest-level intel agents of the black hats would never be able to figure it out. And the most eye-opening part about it is that the white hats knew that they would only get one shot to implement their counter NWO plan or else humanity would have no future and the black hats would kill off 90 percent of the population and enslave the rest as it was so definitively outlined in the infamous Georgia Guidestones.

These granite Guidestones that were erected in 1980 by the globalists and destroyed by the white hats with a vehicle mounted directed energy weapon in 2022 laid out ten guiding principles for humanity living in harmony with nature. However, when you ask the right questions, look past the manipulations and look closer at the intentions and mystery of the stone's creator, you'll see why it was deemed satanic ideology. Whenever something appears to sound good but one way or the other only seems to benefit someone at the cost of someone else's life with zero empathy for that other person, it's likely satanic. These elites are not only pirates and Freemasons, but they are also satanic. Whether they are part of an elite gentlemen's club—such as Bohemian Grove—an elite fraternity—such as the higher echelons of Freemasonry—or part of an elite secret society—such as the Bonesmen or the Illuminati—these people worship demons, such as Baal, Moloch, Baphomet, and, of course, the prince of darkness himself. At the highest levels of power, when these people gather at ceremonies, rituals, and secret meetings, what they consider good for them is not good to anyone else at all.

Reader discretion is advised for this next bit. What if I were to tell you that the evilest things about the world that your mind could possibly fathom WERE ACTUALLY TRUE? For the longest time, these sick people would sacrifice children at many of their gatherings. They would conduct such horrendous and unspeakable acts during rituals at their secret globalist and elitist meetings or getaways like CERN and Epstein Island. They would actually have hunting parties where the children were sent into the wild with no clothing or supplies of any kind while these sick people would hunt them down on horses with weapons or whatever method of their choice, and when captured, they would rape, torture, and sacrifice these children to their demonic gods. Whether it was Baphomet, Baal, Moloch, or Satan himself, these sick bastards believed that the needless and pointless killing of innocent children somehow made them more powerful. Not an easy pill to swallow I know, but it's true!

They even managed to use so-called legitimate agencies such as Planned Parenthood, DHS, and the CIA to make certain operations appear "legal" when behind the scenes they were beyond sinister. Planned Parenthood would gather aborted fetuses and sell them on the black market for people with nefarious intentions, such as organ harvesting and even food manufacturing. DHS would take advantage of their power to take children away from what they considered "bad" parents in the name of protecting the children. But in truth, they would utilize their government powers with the assistance of the corrupt court system, and they would gather as many unadopted children as they could to sell on the black market. The CIA's operations were by far the evilest. They entrenched themselves so deep into the creation of underground laboratories where children were practically stockpiled in cages and experimented on. All for the extraction of an elite drug called adrenochrome.

Adrenochrome is an elitist immortality drug similar to the effects of heroine but with antiaging side effects created by causing terrorizing fear and trauma into young children in order to extract the resulting liquid (adrenochrome) from their pineal gland, which is typically located in the very center of the human head. One could say that's the location of the very essence of the soul. Some say that these children were not only sold to the elite but also traded as part of a deal with higher intelligent beings. But the fact of the matter is that this is why World War III began. It's because human trafficking and child sex slavery have not only surpassed the arms and drug trades like the film *Sound of Freedom* so eloquently says, but it has been happening on an industrial scale beyond what anyone can imagine.

Another factor about adrenochrome that gets overlooked is the fact that there is even a synthetic version of adrenochrome; you may know it as fentanyl. The wide distribution of fentanyl in America has caused countless deaths. One of the most dangerous factors about it is that it can kill you on your first use. And even if you manage to cheat death with your first few uses, it now has you and won't let go until you're dead. Fentanyl is responsible for causing the most drug overdoses in the United States. Particularly because it can be mixed with heroin, cocaine, and can come in pill form. I can definitely attest to its dangers and effects during my time working directly with the homeless in the middle of a tent city as an armed guard. Seeing the grip it had on people and witnessing the long-lasting devastating effects and destructive path it left in its wake whenever it touched the lives of many of the people I came to know and love within the homeless community was utterly heartbreaking.

One of the main things to understand about the black hats was the CIA's sixteen-year plan to destroy America. It started out with installing one of their agents into the presidency in 2008. All the three-letter agencies were informed about this particularly high-value political asset from Chicago, but he wasn't even a United States citizen. He also worked for Saudi intelligence and was being developed to infiltrate the presidency. This asset was Barry Soetoro, otherwise known as Barack Hussein Obama. This sixteen-year plan consisted of eight years of Obama and eight years of Hillary. Soetoro's part in this agenda was to weaken America's influence globally from the inside out one organization at a time. He would do this by first removing good guys from government. Then he would weaken our military by cutting its funding and instead fund terrorist organizations, such as MS13 and ISIS.

He was even responsible for all the out-of-control drone strikes on ISIS's enemies and innocent people in the Middle East. He would leak classified intel and military secrets to China and Russia. He would sell off special access programs. He would fund and nuclearize North Korea and Iran and turn a blind eye to all progress made with a scandal called Uranium 1. He would weaken the NSA by revealing programs, such as X Key Score with the Edward Snowden Leaks.

He would weaken command of generals by ending "Don't ask, don't tell." He would target and weaken the conservative base through the IRS and MSM bias as well as legalize propaganda in the US and give the military industrial complex the green light to conduct psychological operations on American citizens.

He would also pack and stage the Supreme Court, kill NASA space supremacy by ending the space shuttle, and he would relax borders and flood in the illegals to get new democratic voters. I'll personally never forget how he was the first US president I've ever seen in my lifetime to actually negotiate with terrorists. And I'll also never forget how he gloated about being the president that captured bin Laden and then showcased dropping his so-called body into the ocean as if bin Laden were Megatron from the Transformers franchise, especially since it's now known that Osama bin Laden was also a CIA agent closely involved with the Bush family and the 9/11 attacks. But most importantly, let's not forget how the Obama administration had Seal Team Six assassinated either to cover up or possibly retaliate for killing bin Laden or possibly bin Laden's double. But since Bush, Obama, and bin Laden were all affiliated with the CIA, is it really that hard to believe that birds of a feather flock together? And on top of it all, Obama was actually awarded the Nobel Peace Prize for it all. These people really are stupid, sick, and evil.

Obama's insertion into the presidency to destroy America from within was no secret among only the black hats. The white hats knew all about this. But the whites hats also knew that they needed to tread softly and carefully if they were going to thwart the black hat's plan in a way that would not only put an end to certain battles but would ultimately put an end to all pointless and costly wars. In fact, this is exactly how the white hats recognized that the NSA could be used to take down the black hats when it came to having an effective weapon that could be used against them. As a matter of fact, would you believe me if I told you that the white hats were even ready to perform a coup d'état on Barack Obama as soon as he got into office?

Now as memorable as it would have been to read in our history books about the military saving the world for a short moment of time before the cabal would eventually take the world back again, this move would not have had any lasting change and more importantly would have left open an irreversible opportunity to backfire on the white hats and even worse, the world. I could only imagine that the black hats would have retaliated by using the fake news, corrupt courts, and intel agencies in a nefarious way that would have manipulated the already deeply brainwashed population into further believing that certain good guys were "bad" and would have set the white hats back or destroyed them completely. And if the white hats were no more, this book would not exist; you and I would not exist. And for the 10 percent of population, we would have had left after the black hat's plan succeeded. They would have been enslaved in a New World Order that would be so unbearable; death would have become far more desirable than life ever was.

Thank God that the white hats chose a different path and ended up doing the one thing that could ultimately win the war to end all wars. They spoke to Donald J. Trump. Now I already know what you're probably thinking. But before you think that thought, let me just remind you that during Donald Trump's presidency, the deep state and fake news media never advertised or so much as even mentioned anything good Donald Trump ever did. So it's likely that you may already have a skewed perspective on the man to begin with. But let's just remember that when Trump educated the white hats in the military on how they could eradicate the deep state for good, the white hats couldn't refuse. If you've ever done your research on Trump like I have, you'd know that one of the things he did during his time as a businessman was learn who his real friends were when he amounted his enormous wealth.

When his wealth was there and many people who claimed to be his friends were also there, he was shocked to learn who would actually stick by him when his wealth diminished. He said it was never who you'd think it would be and that you could never guess it. This life experience of Donald Trump's birthed the idea to the white hats for a military intelligence sting operation. And Trump's knowledge of the art of war and creation of the art of the deal birthed the idea for the white hats to use the abilities of a savvy businessman to take down USA Inc., get to the root, and lure the enemy out of its dark hiding places and put them into a position of destroying themselves while they think they are winning. All while exposing them little by little to the people until the people are awake enough to ensure that this kind of evil NEVER HAPPENS AGAIN. So while this plan still came at a high cost because there are always casualties of war, it was still far better than the alternative but also would open the door to transitioning us into a new golden age that will last for eons.

As for Hillary Rodham Clinton also known as (Killary Rotten or Rothschild Clinton), an Illuminati grand dame, her job was to orchestrate World War III through the Uranium 1 scandal as well as a number of other means. After this she would revise our constitution after killing our rights and freedoms. She would close US military bases globally. She would then depopulate the planet with an orchestrated mass extinction event that would kill off 90 percent of the population while pocketing billions or even trillions. She would stage mass shootings using MKUltra mind control to scare the public into allowing a repeal of our Second Amendment in order to completely ban the sale of firearms. She would also destroy and censor all alternative media and opposing news outlets by weaponizing FCC censorship. She would then eliminate all the last remaining good guys in government to ensure no resistance or opposition.

She would install corrupt Supreme Court Justices, ensuring that only democratic/liberal legal wins would take place since the Democratic Party has been captured and compromised the longest. As well as having wide open borders to ensure an endless supply of Democratic voters. She would also kill the economy by starving and enslaving the public by locking us down due to a real pandemic for over five years, making us beg for a vaccine that would have killed us off even further as well. She would ensure that the electoral college be completely removed and install rigged voting machines to ensure popular vote only. She would weaken our military assets by completely removing funding.

Then last but surely not least, the worst part is she would ensure that the aristocrats actually pulled all this off to usher in a New World Order, a prison planet, a Great Reset, a fourth industrial revolution of artificial intelligence or full spectrum dominance for the elites.

Killary once told a whistleblower that "it's almost time for the great culling, it's almost time for the useless eaters to be culled." This is actually how these people talked. It was bad enough that a CIA agent was allowed to infiltrate the presidency, but could you imagine if an Illuminati grand dame did? It would be the end of the world as we know it. Thank God she never got in. Because the best part is that ultimately these sick and evil plans would fail because of one simple fact and one simple fact only...THEY NEVER THOUGHT SHE WOULD LOSE!

We will keep their lives short and their minds weak while pretending to do the opposite. We will use our knowledge of science and technology in subtle ways so that they never see what is happening. We will use soft metals, aging accelerators, and sedatives in food and water as well as in the air. They will be covered in poisons wherever they turn. The soft metals will make them lose their minds. We will promise to find a cure from our many funds, and yet we will give them more poison. Chemical poisons will be absorbed through the skin of idiots who believe that certain hygiene and beauty products presented by great actors and musicians will bring eternal youth to their faces and bodies, and through their thirsty and hungry mouths, we will destroy their minds and systems of internal organs and reproduction. However, their children will be born as disabled and deformed, and we will hide this information.
—John Davison Rockefeller, founder
of Standard Oil Company and richest man in modern history

Chapter 4

The White Hats

Shall We Play a Game?

Our movement is about replacing a failed and corrupt political establishment with a new government controlled by you the American people. The Washington establishment and the financial and media corporations that fund it exist for only one reason… to protect and enrich itself. The establishment has trillions of dollars at stake in this election. For those who control the levers of power in Washington and for the global special interests, they partner with these people who don't have your good in mind. Our campaign represents a true existential threat like they haven't seen before. This is not simply another four-year election. This is a crossroads in the history of our civilization that will determine whether or not we the people reclaim control over our government. The political establishment that is trying to stop us is the same group responsible for our disastrous trade deals, massive illegal immigration, economic and foreign policies that have bled our country dry. The political establishment has brought about the destruction of our factories and our jobs as they flee to Mexico, China, and other countries all around the world. It's a global power structure that is responsible for the economic decisions that have robbed our working class, stripped our country of its wealth, and put that money into the pockets of a handful of large corporations and political entities. This is a struggle for the survival of our nation. And this will be our last chance to save it. This election will determine whether we're a free nation or whether we have only the illusion of democracy but are in fact controlled by a small handful of global special interests rigging the system and our system is rigged. This is reality. You know it. They know it. I know it. And pretty much the whole world knows it. The Clinton machine is at the center of this power structure. We've seen this firsthand in the WikiLeaks documents in which Hillary Clinton meets in secret with international banks to plot the destruction of US sovereignty in order to enrich these global financial powers, her special interest friends, and her donors. Honestly, she should be locked up! The most powerful weapon deployed by the Clintons is the corporate media, the press. Let's be clear on one thing…the corporate media in our country is no longer involved in journalism. They're a political special interest no different than any lobbyist or other financial entity with a total political agenda, and the agenda is not for you; it's for themselves. Anyone who challenges their control is deemed a sexist, a racist, a xenophobe. They will lie, lie, lie. The establishment that protects them has engaged in a massive cover-up of widespread criminal activity at the State Department in order to remain in power. Nevertheless, I take all of these slings and arrows gladly for you. I take them so that we can have our country back. The only thing that can stop this corrupt machine is *you*. The only force strong enough to save our country is *us*.

—Donald John Trump's inauguration speech,
forty-fifth and fourty-seventh president of USA
Inc. and nineteenth president of the original
Republic of the United States of America

That was the first time in a very long time that a president of this great nation actually told us the truth. The real truth. When he said that they were not merely transferring power from one administration to another or one party to another but that they were transferring power from Washington, DC, and giving it back to we the people…he wasn't kidding. Fascinatingly enough, however, looking back in hindsight, most of the people who witnessed that speech at the time didn't think much of it. They just thought his words were shiny and appealing for a political candidate to say in order to win an election and become our next president. They had no idea that his speech was military in nature and littered with symbols and dog comms (such as the judge advocate generals or JAG that escorted President Trump to the podium) that if you were smart enough to decipher, you could see past the political jargon and you would know that he was one of the first presidents to ask "we the people" for help.

The black hats and white hats both understood one thing…that without the people on your side, you cannot win this war. Whereas infil-"traitor" Barry Soetoro weaponized the FBI, CIA, DOJ, and a number of other three-letter agencies, President Trump would weaponize the American people. As for the symbolism and dog comms in that speech, you could say it's like when a prisoner of war is being televised by his captors but is blinking in Morse code in order to get a message out to the right people. Thankfully that message was eventually received. But at that time, little did people know that they would become part of a global military and civilian alliance that would change the course of history forever and bear witness to the largest global military intelligence sting operation in the history of humanity.

This would be introduced by an epic phenomena known as Q-coded messages and drops on an intel board released by the white hats in the US Military in 2017 onto public forums, such as 4-Chan and 8-Kun, that was like them throwing "we the people" a metaphorical life raft to prepare us for "the storm" to come if you will. This life raft was the key to weaponizing the American people against the cabal. There were roughly five thousand Q drops to be decoded and analyzed. But what was most genius about these drops is the extraordinary way they would mostly ask questions. These questions would then inspire the reader (a.k.a. Anon) to research and critically think for themselves in order to find the answers organically. Two things that Anons always found incredibly mind-blowing was first that when using time stamps from dates and times of certain memes, posts, videos, and photos from social media about current events, it would sync and perfectly match the drop as if Q can either predict the future or is completely in control of world events. And second is learning how deep the rabbit hole really goes when it comes to the amount of pure evil that actually exists in the world.

These drops would cause the reader to research history, politics, geopolitics, military, science, and even the Bible. At one point, Gen. Michael Flynn announced that they had an army of digital soldiers that would utilize social media to take over the idea of information. These digital soldiers otherwise known as "Anons" would provide the fuel, knowledge, and tools for the people to join forces with the white hats for a first ever MIL-CIV alliance to crush the cabal with the one weapon they could never stop…truth and exposure. With Donald Trump secretly (CIC, commander in chief) combined with the organic seed planted of "we the people" slowly waking up more and more by the day, this movement would use the powers of life against the powers of death. And what exactly is the power of life? It grows!

The fake news always referred to this movement as "QANON: THE SECRET CULT OF CRAZY RIGHT-WINGED CONSPIRACY THEORISTS TERRORISTS EXTREMISTS WHO BELIEVE THAT DONALD TRUMP WILL SAVE THE WORLD FROM A SECRET CULT OF SATANIC ELITIST BLOODSUCKING PEDOPHILES WHO ARE TRYING TO TAKE OVER THE WORLD!" This always made me laugh when I heard them say that over and over because I always thought, *Well, yeah*. Even Donald Trump once told a black hat interviewer when she mentioned what QANON was, "Is that such a bad thing?" The black hats and the fake news were always really good about projecting onto their enemies the very thing that they themselves are guilty of. This is a classic yet predictable tactic taken straight out of the communist playbook. One could always tell when the fake news knew nothing of what they were talking about because true digital soldiers and patriots knew that there is Q and there are Anons, but there is no such thing as "QANON."

Who Q really is, was something that no one ever wanted to believe at the time, and if you told them, they thought you were crazy. You see, no other president, and I would even say man, has ever been as loved and hated as much as Donald Trump. There was no in-between or gray area. You either loved him or you hated him. I always loved him because of how much of a boss he was, always firing people on his show *The Apprentice*, guest starring on *The Fresh Prince of Bel Air* or being a special guest on the *WWE*. I thought how refreshing it was to finally have a truly honest president who doesn't take crap from anyone for a change. Not to mention that he's the first president whose net worth went down because he never took one red cent from the government. Of course, he was only hated because ol' silver-tongued Barry Soetoro weaponized the three-letter agencies and the fake news against him. Why do you think the news was always so biased? That is because 99 percent of the news stations were liberal, with the exception of Fox News so they could at least appear fair or balanced. In fact, the CIA actually employed over 50 percent of the fake corrupt news media, and because of that, you better believe that all assets were deployed to take him down.

Everything from completely fabricated stories, scandals, false impeachments, hoaxes, conspiracy theories, deep fakes, and even doubles. Not to mention they never talked about anything good he ever did. It was round-the-clock, nonstop fake story after story, talk show after morning show after day show after night show of malicious attacks on Donald Trump. Why was the media and the left so die-hard dedicated to destroying him? And why would Donald Trump be so dedicated to carrying on and marching forward even though he was attacked by the media nonstop? He didn't do it for the money; he was already a billionaire. He didn't do it for the fame; he was already incredibly famous. He could've easily retired to spend quality time with his beloved family. But instead he chose to take on the two most difficult jobs in America: president of the United States and America's most wanted man. As a matter of fact, here's one the media has never told you because their handlers were likely responsible. Did you know that he's had over thirty assassination attempts on his life and his family's lives? The fake news never wanted to mention that one, did they? One thing is for sure, for the longest time, I always wondered what his haters would think if they ever found out what he was really up to while they were preoccupied with hating him so much. Well, if you still don't want to know, then why the heck are you reading this book? But if you do want to know, then allow me to educate you…

The moment he came down that shiny escalator was when "they" knew they were in trouble. That's when "they" knew he was going to "drain the swamp" of all the evil swamp creatures. That's when "they" knew for the first time that someone who was not part of their club of sick and evil corruption was actually there to destroy them. And not only could he do that, but he also would. After being inaugurated, one of the first things Donald Trump did was create Executive Orders 13773 and 13848, which essentially enabled him to utilize the entire might of the US Military to arrest and seize all assets of anyone caught interfering with US elections, abusing human rights, crimes against humanity, or human trafficking domestically or abroad. And because the white hats already knew who was one of the guiltiest culprits of this, another one of the first things he did was declare war on the CIA. You may as well consider all mainstream media a CIA asset fully owned and controlled. This is why many of the "sleepers," or "normies" as we would call them, never had any idea about the world tour Trump took in his first week of office. And the most curious thing about these executive orders, was that Joe Biden never reversed them

Instead of the fake news reporting on the good things Donald Trump was doing, they were too busy bashing him and fabricating scandals, such as the Russia, Russia, Russia hoax, in order to get him out of office. But little did the fake news know that Trump was secretly organizing a global alliance actually called the Alliance to coordinate a massive takedown of all the cabal's Mafias, secret societies, and intricately widespread criminal networks and crime syndicates all across the globe. A massive undertaking because, of course, every country has their own deep state to deal with. China has the CCP, Russia has Ukraine, and both the state of Israel and the United States have the three-letter agencies, Mossad, Hamas, and the Khazarian Mafia. So while the normies and lefties were too busy allowing Donald Trump to live rent-free in their heads, they were completely unaware that Trump, through executive orders, vowed to completely eradicate human trafficking from the earth, abolish the IRS and Federal Reserve, returning the gold and government back to the people like Robin Hood, and finally implement NESARA/GESARA once and for all. So when you think about how big of a job that is, try thinking about what it would actually take to achieve it and then think about whether you believe it or not or like it or not; it's been happening.

When Trump conducted his world tour, every single government on earth, absolutely all of them, capitulated to him. He made sure to go to Saudi Arabia first so that he could immediately tackle the issue of adrenochrome. The man to take down for this was Saudi Arabian Crown Prince Al Waleed bin Talal Al Saud. Many of Saudi Arabia's people and officials did not like him. They knew he was up to no good from the beginning, and they were right. This was because most people draw the line when it comes to children. He was involved with the thirteen families, human trafficking, and the intelligence agencies. In fact, with his affiliations with Mossad and the CIA, it was him that selected Barry Soetoro to infiltrate America's presidency with a CIA agent. Trump had the white hats sweep up and arrest Al Waleed and many of his closest men. Mohammed bin Salman who despised Al Waleed would take his place as crown prince. And then the very next day, the crown prince and the king publicly submitted control of Saudi Arabia to Donald J. Trump. They celebrated this publicly with their extravagant sword dance ritual. And in this ritual, only the king holds the sword.

Before it was hidden or possibly scrubbed from the Internet, I definitely saw the photos and videos of Trump holding the king's sword with a big smile on his face. After handing over the keys to Saudi Arabia, Trump and Salman became very good friends. Salman would then become part of the Q Plan. He would do this by not only cleaning out any remaining trash in Saudi Arabia, but he was also given the Trump card over all the big tech companies who were also a huge part of the black hat's New World Order. The deep state was not happy about this, so in retaliation, an attempt was made on Mohammed bin Salman's life while he was in Las Vegas visiting America. While the attempt was unsuccessful, it unfortunately resulted in the deaths of sixty-plus people and went down in history as the largest mass shooting ever to be committed by one man. Of course, the deep state used the tragedy of this incident to push more gun control, blaming it on bump stocks. When the truth is that man was a well-funded agent sent to hunt down Salman, and when he was unsuccessful, he still followed his orders to take out as many useless eaters as possible. These people are sick!

After Saudi Arabia, Trump immediately went to Israel where he met with all the leaders of Israel to discuss Israel's capitulation. However, they were not quite ready to sign Israel over. But Trump did demonstrate his power by visiting the Wailing Wall with Melania. Many people became angry because they thought Trump had sided with the Zionists, but he didn't. In fact, Trump stayed one more day so that he could make it perfectly clear that the United States would recognize Jerusalem as the eternal capital of Israel and that with their capitulation, he would be moving the US Embassy from Tel Aviv to Jerusalem. Once Trump laid everything out on the table and discussed his plan to eradicate human trafficking from the earth, they, too, became part of the Q Plan and the Alliance.

Trump's next destination was definitely one for the record books (you're welcome) and my absolute favorite...the Vatican. In 1823, the Rothschild family took over all financial operations of the Catholic Church. Trump didn't go to the Vatican to make pals with Pope Francis and let him in on the Q Plan or join the Alliance. He went there to blackmail the pope and return to the people what is rightfully theirs. All Trump did was hand him a thick folder from a table with a mountain of folders and told Pope Francis to take a good look. These folders contained tons and tons and tons of evidence of the Vatican's involvement and orchestration of child sex trafficking. There were even photos of the pope as part of the Red Shoe Club. It's a secret club of elite Satan-worshipping psychopaths that get their kicks from the torture and raping of children. And we all know what Jesus said about what should happen to whomever dares to harm His little ones.

Trump gave the pope two very simple options, either he could sign a few documents for him or he and his minions could be completely exposed to the world for the sick, evil, twisted monsters that they are. The pope was so caught off guard in such shock and disdain about their meeting that Trump stayed one more day to ensure that the pope could sleep on it and really think about what would happen if he didn't sign those documents over to Trump. So the very next day, the pope signed over all the documents Trump had asked for including the papal bull, making Donald J. Trump the new executor exchequer of the Federal Reserve as well as every nation's treasury on the entire planet. Now with the deed to the earth in hand, believe it or not, that one signature secretly made Donald J. Trump the richest man in all of known human history.

Possessing the papal bull was crucial because the skeletons in the closet of the Vatican are massive! Not only did the Vatican have tons of hidden demonic symbolism throughout, but deep underneath the Vatican, there were also tunnels used for child trafficking and tunnels of demonic statues and relics that definitely did not represent heavenly things, not to mention the massive underground libraries of lost and coveted books of truths and our hidden history, including the *Emerald Tablet*. Can you imagine what true knowledge has been hidden from us? And can you imagine the look of surprise on the faces of white hat Special Forces teams when they found miles and miles of deep tunnels containing at least a quintillion's worth of stolen gold and treasure? It took 650 cargo airplanes to retrieve all the gold from the Vatican.

After becoming the new deed holder of the earth (yes, you heard that correctly!), Donald Trump immediately went to Brussels to have a fine chat with the United Nations, the European Union, and NATO. Trump made sure to be extra late to this meeting because he wanted to show who was in charge. After making these sick evil globalists piss themselves waiting for Trump to arrive, he then laid everything down for them nice and thick. He only needed to remind them that "WE HAVE IT ALL!" And if they don't play ball, "DECLASS!" It doesn't leave you much choice if you're a baby-killing, Satan-worshipping psychopath. So they capitulated, of course.

One thing Anons and I definitely understand is that the scale of lies we've all been brainwashed with is so mind-bending and paradigm-shifting because learning the truth was basically learning that many of the people you thought were good are actually bad. And the ones you thought were bad are actually good. Also the ones you thought were alive are dead and the ones you thought were dead are actually alive.

This goes for many politicians, CEOs, celebrities, and leaders that many of us looked up to or even idolized throughout the years. I was definitely heartbroken when I learned who was who. Yes, Anons and patriots have been going through this since the beginning of COVID-19, and for some, it's much longer, but I digress. Trump wrote the book on the art of the deal, but he was also playing 5-D chess and using the art of war and game theory. Tactics such as "appear weak when you are strong," "strong when you are weak," "become your enemy," "don't alert the public, you are at war until the war has been won," along with many others were used. Many people I've spoken to who hate Trump always say the same thing… that he's racist and stupid. But they can never show me a single clip of him ever saying anything racist, only articles. Not to mention if these people only understood the act he's playing and how much of a genius he actually is.

Here's a fun fact the fake news never cared to mention. Did you know that Trump is the first westerner to ever set foot inside of the Forbidden City in China? President Xi Jinping was very good pals with Trump and was indeed made part of the Alliance because the People's Republic of China had their own deep state to deal with which was, of course, the Chinese Communist Party. And Taiwan was always a major hub for human trafficking that needed to be dealt with in one way or the other. Trump was also the first westerner to step across the DMZ in North Korea to shake hands with Kim Jong Un. Q once mentioned in a drop that some information must remain classified till the end. That Kim is not actually running North Korea, that he is only an actor in the play. If people knew who the director behind North Korea was, they would riot, revolt, and reject. I wonder if that's why North Korea has always been such a hell on earth for so long. I think the CIA had something to do with it. I'll let you decide on that one. And, of course, also part of the Alliance is Putin of Russia. Not sure if we're on the fifth or sixth Putin by now, but what I do know is that when Putin handed the soccer ball over to Trump saying "The ball is in your court," it was definitely meant to be symbolic of events to come.

One of the dead giveaways to me about Russia being part of the white hats has always been their coat of arms. It's a shield with the image of a white knight on a horse trampling over and thrusting a spear into the head of a serpent. You can't ask for better symbology than that. Trump also paid a visit to the three powers that represent the triple-sided, all-seeing eye on our fake currency's pyramid. This is known as the Pindar. This is why Trump visited the queen of England and was seen walking in front of her and then stopped. He did that because that was a signal to us that he was putting a stop to England's financial hold on us and the US corporation. This Pindar was ruled by the queen of England, the queen of Holland, and the head of the Illuminati who are now all gone thanks to President Trump. A double of the queen was used for later optics. Also gone is Dun & Bradstreet, the world's creditor for all major corporations. Trump dissolved it, leaving only a shadowy digital footprint for showcasing the illusion of existence for transitional purposes. Some monsters are simply too evil to negotiate with and needed to be executed, eradicated, or dissolved as soon as humanly possible.

Personally, without a doubt, during this war, convincing people about the existence of the white hats and that there were actually good people fighting for us behind the scenes has definitely been a lost cause. So much so that it got to a point where I would become like Q, and instead of telling people the truth, I would just show them. Even some fellow patriots were hard to convince. So who were the white hats? First and foremost, Donald Trump was always Q+. This was confirmed when an Anon on the intel board wanted confirmation from Q that the white hat military proudly serves at the behest of the real president and commander in chief, Donald J. Trump. So how did Q confirm this? By having Trump say in his next public speech any outlandish code word that the Anon could come up with. This particular Anon wanted it to be a code word that President Trump wouldn't likely say unless he was clearly instructed to. Therefore, the code word that the Anon chose to have President Trump say was none other than "tippy top." And so the next speech that Donald Trump gave just so happened to be on the same day the request was made, Easter Sunday that is. And Q even managed to make it happen within the same hour. So while Trump was standing there with Melania and the Easter Bunny, Trump gleefully wished we the people of America a "tippy top Easter!" He even went a little overboard saying the words "tippy top" a lot. Aside from many of the incredible Q proofs and decodes that Anons figured out, in my opinion, this was the proof that "tippy topped" the cake. How many coincidences until it's mathematically impossible? And because of this amazing proof, my hat goes off to the curious Anon now known as "Tippy Top Patriot."

So who is Q? On the entire planet, there are only two hundred naval pilots that have Q clearance and are Q capable of carrying a nuclear weapon. No one else can do that. And since Donald Trump has been CIC and Q+ throughout this entire war, you better believe he's always had the football. Trump was secretly inaugurated as the president and commander in chief of the original republic of the United States of America in March of 2021 just shortly after Joe Robinette Biden's double (actor Arthur Roberts) was inaugurated as Resident and CEO of the now bankrupt and dismantled UNITED STATES corporation. This was apparent to Anons and patriots in the know because Biden's cannon salute was held at Arlington National Cemetery with only a three-cannon salute instead of four, just as the white hat's way of mocking the black hats. The mocking also continued when fake Joe Biden left in his motorcade and the military turned their backs on Biden.

This was quite the sight to witness because normally if you did something like that, you would be barred and court-martialed. But they weren't because of what was really going on. The real Joe Biden was executed by the military in 2018 for treason and his crimes against children. Q is six military intelligence agencies led by the president of the United States of America. Some of these include the secret army of Northern Virginia, DOE, ARCYBER, and Space Force, and it's all being helped by one very special man. He has been side by side with President Trump throughout this whole journey and has been serving as our vice president of the original republic throughout this entire war. He was thought to be long dead, but his death was thwarted by the white hats and has been under military protection ever since. While President Trump has been playing his part as the public face for everyone to love or hate, this man has been slowly guiding Anons and patriots underground throughout alternative media, such as Rumble, while concealing his identity the entire time. This very special man is none other than John F. Kennedy Jr.

> My fellow Americans, over the course of the next several days, you will undoubtedly realize that we are taking back our great country (the land of the free) from the evil tyrants that wish to do us harm and destroy the last remaining refuge of shining light. On POTUS's order, we have initiated certain fail-safes that shall safeguard the public from the primary fallout which is slated to occur 11.3 upon the arrest announcement of Mr. Podesta (actionable 11.4). Confirmation (to the public) of what is occurring will then be revealed and will not be openly accepted. Public riots are being organized in serious numbers in an effort to prevent the arrest and capture of more senior public officials. On POTUS's order, a state of temporary military control will be actioned and special ops carried out. False leaks have been made to retain several within the confines of the United States to prevent extradition and special operator necessity. Rest assured the safety and well-being of every man, woman, and child of this country is being exhausted in full. However, the atmosphere within the country will unfortunately be divided as so many have fallen for

the corrupt and evil narrative that has long been broadcasted. We will be initiating the Emergency Broadcast System (EBS) during this time in an effort to provide a direct message (avoiding the fake news) to all citizens. Organizations and/or people that wish to do us harm during this time will be met with swift fury—certain laws have been pre-lifted to provide our great military the necessary authority to handle and conduct these operations (at home and abroad).

—Q Drop 34, posted November 1, 2017

Chapter 5

The Secret Space Program

Some Things Must Remain Classified to the Very End

Right now there are 131 active deep underground military bases in the United States. There's 1,477 of them worldwide. Each one has an average cost of seventeen to nineteen billion dollars. Each one used to take a year to two years to build. And now they're capable of building a couple of them a year with sophisticated methods. My colleague, Al Bielek, has actually been on some of the high-speed railways, the magnetic levitation trains that connect all the deep underground military bases within the United States. He's been on a MACH-2 train that floats off of a single rail three fourth of an inch. This is what you call high tech. We have nothing like this on the surface. Groom Lake is where the infamous Area 51, S4, S2, and the CIA base that was originally a bombing range and nuclear test site has become the most secret base in the United States. It employs over eighteen thousand workers who work in twelve-hour shifts, and most of them work in the cover of darkness. We built out nine deep underground military bases each with an average capacity of holding a city underground. Roughly 4 1/4 cubic miles hollowed out underground. They have nuclear boring machines that literally vitrify and melt the rock with a very sophisticated laser that reduces the rock to a powder and then melts it. These mega bases are gobbling up our gross national product. Right now

we're spending 28 percent of the gross national product on building
underground bases solely. That doesn't count for the defense
budget, that doesn't count for the spare parts budget, it doesn't
account for any of that at all. The black budget is dead, dead wrong.
It sidesteps the United States Congress and its constitution of its
people and says you're a bunch of morons that don't need to know.
A need-to-know basis was an executive order written during the
Eisenhower era right after the created 1954 treaty and is treasonous
and illegal in this country and should be overturned and abolished.
Alien takeover is a serious threat. Kept totally out of the public
view, off the surface, I'm sure the underground bases, without
question, are being used as places to house alien takeover. Alien
takeover means the implementation of a one-world government.
—Phil Schneider, Area 51 whistleblower

Would you believe me if I told you that we are most definitely not
alone in the universe? Would you agree that we no longer need the
government to announce to us that aliens exist because collectively as
a human race, we already have more-than-enough evidence to prove
it ourselves? Would you believe me if I told you that non-terrestrial
beings that many believe are too far away or too fantastical or outrageous to exist actually do exist much closer than we think? What if
that's true? And what if they have had a secret influence on human
history for far longer than we think? Would you agree that those who
don't know history are doomed to repeat it? Is that perhaps why I'm
writing this book?

Is there a metaphorical ant farm with entities on the outside
controlling things and I'm merely an ant that got a glimpse of what
those entities are and are merely trying to share with my fellow ants
what I've seen? Or would everything that happened during my brief
blink of an eye amount of time I got to spend here in this matrix of
an ant farm just get lost in translation? Is it possible that the depths
of pure evil in modern times originated from otherworldly beings? If
you properly understood what Phil Schneider said about aliens being
real and that they had a real agenda for us and that they've been

collaborating with our government in Area 51, could that have really been possible? If so, where did it all begin?

Exactly what is Operation Paperclip and Operation High Jump? Of all the countries and diversity of peoples of the world, why would aliens contact the Nazis as early as 1939 right before World War 2? And why would destiny or fate have it that this race of aliens would be nefarious like the Nazis but far worse? How would all the whistleblowers of the SSP come to refer to these beings as the Saurians or the Draco? Is it really possible that when the Draco contacted the Nazis, they shared technology with them, such as de Glock (the Bell) or anti-gravitational mechanisms that could attach to their submarines in order to travel to the moon and beyond? Wouldn't a submarine be the perfect vehicle for traveling in outer space since it's completely sealed and capable of submersing under immense pressure in the deepest of water? If so, why would the Nazis establish a secret base in Antarctica known as New Shwabia in 1939? Does it have anything to do with the leaked footage of US Marines being deployed to explore the Antarctic pyramids more recently discovered by researchers in 2012? Or what if perhaps there's a main entrance point in Antarctica that leads into the massive underground tunnels and caverns that the Draco have inhabited for thousands or maybe even millions of years? If that's true, is it possibly connected to any of the 1,477 DUMBs that are hidden underground throughout the earth? If the Draco traded technology with the Nazis, then what did the Nazis give the Draco in return?

Can it really be true that in 1945 via Operation Paperclip that the Nazis secretly brought hundreds of Nazi scientists into the United States to be hired by the military industrial complex? In 1946, did ADM Richard Byrd really lead an expedition of over four thousand men named Operation High Jump to seek out New Shwabia along with other Antarctica bases? Did his personal journal really speak on finding the entrance to a different world filled with extraterrestrial technologies, green forests, and large mammals? Because if he didn't see such things, then why did he tell Chilean Newspaper *El Mercurio* that in the event of a new war, the United States would be facing highly sophisticated craft that can fly from one pole to the other at incredible speeds? Is this perhaps why all topographical scans of this mysterious void have always been completely missing? What exactly did Admiral Byrd find down there?

Whatever he found must have been pretty spectacular because why else would a dozen nations agree to sign the Antarctic Treaty in 1959 to make it illegal for anyone to travel south of the sixtieth parallel without government authorization? Is it really that crazy to believe that the US military industrial complex was compromised by the infiltrating Nazis who acquired Draco reptilian technology? Haven't you ever heard the expression "if you can't beat 'em, join 'em"? Why else would American scientist and SSP whistleblower William Thompkins work so passionately to share his experiences building UFOs at the Douglas Aircraft Company with the whole world in his book? Did he actually take part in firing over a thousand rounds at UFOs in the Battle of Los Angeles as a naval intelligence officer in 1942? Can we really believe that it's a coincidence that during this secretive boom of UFO reverse engineering from the 1940s and beyond, Lockheed Martin just coincidentally happened to launch its Advanced Development Programs (ADP) division Skunkworks at known locations, such as the United States Air Force Plant 42 in Palmdale, California, and the Nevada Test Site?

If the military industrial complex knew how to reverse engineer much of this alien technology, then what exactly is Project Blue Beam? If according to one anonymous whistleblower who was stationed at an underground military base near Boulder, Colorado, in 1986 was exposed to a stealth bomber by his commanding officer that was not even real but had him completely convinced it was, could it be true that black hat scientists have been perfecting this holographic technology since the early 1950s? Was the Phoenix Lights Craft witnessed by over ten thousand people really the first successful grand scale Project Blue Beam test ever conducted on the American People? And did the black hats conceive of the idea to do such a thing from when Orson Welles unleashed his *War of the Worlds* book on the radio to the American public in 1938? Was this really a time when the American public was so fooled by media that many went into a mass panic in droves because they were convinced that Martians were really attacking?

Did the cabal really develop Project Blue Beam to use as the last resort and crescendo of their ultimate plan of depopulation for humanity if all other plans failed? Did they really want humanity to be fooled into believing that nefarious aliens invaded Earth when in truth it would be real military aircraft inflicting actual damage but disguised as UFOs in order to pull off the ultimate false flag on the unsuspecting public? And did they actually believe that once this trick was pulled off on the global population in 2024, they would be able to immediately assemble a one-world government and establish a New World Order without any resistance from the people? If that was their plan all along, then did that plan include an awake population that has been woken up by the white hats and have been inspired to ask questions and think for themselves? If the black hats were in control when Project Blue Beam was created but then the white hats began waking up the world about what's really going on, who do you think is in control now?

What about the moon? Is it really true that Neil Armstrong and Buzz Aldrin actually did land on the moon but what happened there and what they saw was something else entirely than what we've been told? Were they really under NDAs not to say anything about what they really saw? Was what they saw really so outrageous that no one would believe the only two American heroes with real experience of first setting foot on the moon because the media would claim it's just another conspiracy theory? If so, then how come Neil Armstrong became somewhat of a recluse after the moon landing? Was he merely a man of such integrity that he simply refused to be put into a position where he would have to lie to the public about what he saw? Or was he already put into an unthinkable position where if he did speak out about what he saw his wife and children would all be killed? If that's true, then does that mean that when Neil Armstrong told mission control that the first thing he saw when he first stepped foot on the Sea of Tranquility crater was a fleet of large spacecraft parked around the crater watching their every move was also true? Considering Neil Armstrong was a decent artist, how come on July 20, 1969, Neil Armstrong felt compelled to draw a very detailed sketch of precisely what he saw that day?

Considering everything that happened in Antarctica decades earlier, is it really that hard to believe that the percentage of Nazis involved with Antarctica became a breakaway civilization and actually made progress to the moon and perhaps even built bases on the dark side? Is it also that hard to believe that during this time, the cabal was in control and simply commanded the CIA to classify all audio and video evidence of the incident above top secret and then simply cover it up with lies? Don't we already know the capability of movie magic? Do you really think the black hats were not capable of implementing movie magic into the news and mainstream media? Could it be true that when William Thompkins described the evidence of hundreds of Draco standing underneath their crafts and watching Neil and Buzz, those same Draco reptilians have been sculpted and depicted over and over again in ancient relics, hieroglyphics, and statues all throughout human history on this planet? Is that just another coincidence or is that a clear connection?

Haven't many people seen the connections clearly made on the History Channel? Why did William Thompkins say that our moon is a vehicle for them and our planet is actually their laboratory? That would explain why we're only able to clearly see one side of the moon but not the other, wouldn't it? So is it really that hard to believe that the terminology "conspiracy theorist" was created by the CIA in order to discredit anyone who challenged their authority or narrative and make it so that only what they say is true and everyone who says otherwise is just plain crazy? Is it a coincidence that the CIA used predictive programming to always paint themselves as the good guys in most movies and television?

Were you aware that we now know for a fact that the moon is actually hollow? Why else did the moon reverberate like a bell for over an hour after the Apollo 12 crew jettisoned the lunar module during its ascent stage causing it to crash into the moon on November 20, 1969? And since we know for a fact that it crashed about forty miles from the Apollo landing site and created an artificial moon quake with shocking characteristics, is it really that hard to believe it's hollow? So if this is true, wouldn't it be impossible for the moon to be hollow naturally? Would you believe me if I told you that there was actually a time in our ancient past when the moon wasn't even there? If not, then why do the ancient calendars created by the Tiwanaku in Bolivia tell us otherwise? And why do we hear about the same thing from Greek authors, such as Aristotle, and Roman authors, such as Ovid, write about a group of people called the Procelenes who lived in Arcadia before there was a moon in the heavens?

Is there really archaeological evidence that suggests that the moon came into Earth's orbit around twelve thousand years ago? Is it also true that not only did African Zulu legends tell of the moon being hollow but that it was inhabited and brought here by entities described to be humanoid with scaly skin? Doesn't it sound like they're describing the Draco? Why else would African Zulu legends describe this forgotten time when there was no moon as having no seasons and the earth being a beautiful, lush place abundant with life when the entire planet was perpetually engulfed by a canopy of water vapor? Is that why they described only being able to see the sun through a watery mist? And why would they explain that the water vapor canopy fell to the earth as a cataclysm of rain when the moon was put into place in the earth's orbit? If your mind is as open as I hope it is by this point, wouldn't that actually explain the rain for forty days and forty nights in Noah's story in the Bible?

What if the earth got thrown off its axis during the moon's placement and caused the earth to have more chaotic tides and tidal waves? If there was no connection or effect that the moon had on the earth, then why would the Zulu also say that before the moon's arrival women did not menstruate? And why would the Zulu, along with many other African tribes, say that the moon was built far, far away by an ancient reptilian race and then placed here on earth to keep a close watch on people? Does that perhaps explain why we're only able to see one side of the moon? Is that why they also said the moon was their mothership that they used to escape to during the great flood and also used as a hub to manipulate countless other cosmic events, such as mass extinctions from a place of complete safety? As outrageous as these ancient and tribal accounts may seem about the moon, doesn't it actually explain a lot about the modern accounts about the moon? Doesn't it explain why the moon gives us evidence of being older than the earth and even our solar system? Doesn't it explain why the moon is the only object in our solar system that orbits another object in an absolute perfect circle and even creates perfectly timed lunar and solar eclipses?

Doesn't this also explain why out of the three distinct layers within the moon's crust, the outer layer is the densest material if it were to be considered the hull of a massive spacecraft? Wouldn't this also explain why little to no water has ever been found on the moon's surface and yet there is evidence that it does exist deep inside? Wouldn't the idea of the moon being an artificial satellite also explain how the photographic evidence of very large straight-lined trails and pathways left by machinery to hollow out the moon would still be there today? Is it possible that moon quakes are not only caused by the stress of the earth's gravitational pull but also caused by artificial constructs giving way or collapsing on the inside throughout its long lifespan? Wouldn't this also explain the photographic evidence of gas clouds coming from the inside of the moon as a byproduct of artificial equipment within the interior? And how do you explain many of the other curious findings that we have photographic evidence of such as one of the most incredible findings on the lunar surface we've ever found called the Tower along with tons of other artificial structures and remnants? What other secrets have they been hiding from us?

Why is it so hard to believe that government agencies like NASA have not told us the whole truth about the moon when all government agencies have a history of concealing groundbreaking information from the general public? Is there a good reason perhaps why my good friend Julie Ann Hanson-Luckett, MS, an aerospace engineer who developed equipment for solar particle events, informed me that the staff at NASA are highly intelligent but super compartmentalized like the military? Is there perhaps a good reason she mentioned that when Obama was in office and commanded focus on Mars, there was good busy worker bee morale among the employees, but as soon as Trump took office and commanded focus on the moon, everyone began freaking out as if NASA hasn't been there since the cover-up? Is there a good reason there haven't been any human missions to the moon since 1969? Is that also why so many conspiracy theories have surfaced about the moon landing being faked and even about *Challenger*? Are the black hats responsible for all this too? Why else is it that whenever evidence or claims come up that are contradictory to what we've been told, it automatically gets censored, shutdown, or labeled as conspiracy theory?

Didn't Julian Assange release through WikiLeaks evidence of clear-as-day lost footage and cutscenes of the faked moon landing being filmed in the Nevada desert? Wouldn't one think to ask why the government went after Julian Assange so hard until they saw that his evidence could expose them and what kind of problems could it have posed to NASA if they didn't cover it up and instead revealed the radio transmissions of Neil and Buzz when they actually went to the moon and encountered the Draco? Are we even really expected to believe that the Draco are the only alien race the government has been hiding from us? And are we also expected to believe that there's no connection to these extraterrestrial races to our ancient past? Haven't you heard the term "the writing is on the wall"?

Why has ancient alien archaeology shown us that an extraterrestrial race called the "Anunnaki" came to Earth many centuries ago to create the human race? Doesn't the data show that the ancient Sumerians are direct descendants of that race? And aren't the Sumerians the oldest known civilization from Mesopotamia which would be located in modern-day Iraq today? If they would have us believe that Atlantis only came from the imagination of Plato, then why has a UK-based group off the coast of Spain found evidence of the lost civilization? What if the moon actually brought humanity itself and populated the islands of Lemur and Atlantis? And what if after both of these islands sank, those people scattered around the earth to make up all the different races that we've become today? Is there more to ancient Iraq then they've been telling us?

Is there possibly enough evidence for us to assume that perhaps there is an alien connection to human trafficking? If we already know from the mountains of evidence about the Draco giving the

Nazis technology, why would it be so hard to believe that the Draco would want humans to experiment on and do all kinds of nefarious things to? Could they want humans to feed on or breed with? Would they perhaps be on the verge of extinction without us? Could it really be true that that's why William Thompkins said that the deal made between the Draco and the Nazis was to ultimately enslave every man, woman, and child? Would that explain why over eight million children have gone missing every year without a trace just in the United States and why human trafficking has gone completely out of control all over the world and reached an industrial scale? Where and when did human trafficking really begin anyway? Can we really believe that throughout all human history the only ones the Draco contacted to spread their evil ways was the Nazis?

If we look deeper in lost history, don't we find that there were other groups effected by the Draco? What about Khazaria between AD 100 and AD 950 or better known today as modern-day Ukraine? Is this really one of the first times and places that the Draco were able to create real human-reptilian hybrids or even discovered their ability to shape-shift into human-looking beings? Is it really true that all European royal families have Khazarian origin? Is this why one of the most incredibly evil societies to ever emerge took root in Khazaria? Did Khazaria really develop into a nation of road bandits, robbers, thieves, rapists, and murderers because they were ruled by an evil king who was a master of ancient Babylonian black arts, black magic, and had occult oligarchs who served as his court?

Considering that we know how the surrounding nations including Russia knew Khazaria to be an evil state, did the Russian czar really give the Khazarian king an ultimatum because of the numerous complaints they received from their citizens as well as all the surrounding countries? As we know, religion was everything in ancient times, so when given three options to adopt Islam, Judaism, or Christianity, why did Khazaria choose Judaism and promise to the confederacy of nations they would follow its teachings but then secretly practice ancient Babylonian black magic and secret Satanism? Did they really secretly perform occult ceremonies of child sacrifice where they would bleed them out, drink their blood, and eat their hearts?

Since the deepest secret of the ancient Babylonian dark arts was that it was all based in Baal worship, is it really that hard to believe that whenever they killed people from surrounding countries they learned how to look like them, steal their identities, and become masters of disguise as a result? And since the Khazarian king used a blended religion of Judaism and Satanism called Talmudism to fool the czar, considering their history of disguise and deceit, would it really be too hard to believe that this reptilian originated evil along with its practices has spread to other secret societies and elite groups throughout the globe and throughout history? Has that darkness even managed to live on through secret societies and even certain deep-rooted politicians today? We've all heard that Satan has ruled the earth for eons, could this be one way how? Could Satan perhaps have ruled our planet since the ancient Sumerians and the Annunaki?

What about the *Emerald Tablet*? Do these ancient tablets really date back to around 36,000 BC, predating any of our religious writings? Did an ancient Annunaki deity or being from Atlantis named "Thoth" really gave us language and mathematics by giving us these mysterious ancient tablets directly? If most other ancient teachings were written by scribes of kings and emperors, then why were these tablets written and authored directly by Thoth himself, saying that he was guiding us back into the Golden Age of Light? Is he really the bringer of knowledge and wisdom to humanity and Thoth is even where we get the word "thought" from? Were the Annunaki really capable of developing technologies that enabled them to live for many thousands of years? And according to the *Emerald Tablet*, was Thoth really the architect who created all the ancient pyramids on the entire planet?

If not, why were many of the teachings from the Bible saying many of the exact same things when put side by side even when the *Emerald Tablet* predate the Bible by tens of thousands of years? And why is it that when you research further into the words of Jesus, whose name is really "Yeshua," you'll not only discover the gospel of the holy twelve but also the forgotten time period of Yeshua's life when he lived in Egypt, Tibet, and India where he learned mystic healing arts as a student of the mystery schools? If the *Emerald Tablet* was believed to be hidden in the archives of the forbidden library in the Vatican, but we now know more recently of how the white hats have secretly gained control over the Vatican, then who do you think is in possession of the *Emerald Tablet* today? More curiously however, if according to 2 Timothy 4:3-4 in the holy bible that a time would come when people would turn away from sound doctrine and seek out false teachers and fables, is it perhaps more likely true that the emerald tablet and the mythology behind Thoth the Atlantean is a completely fake teaching created by science fiction writer and brokered salesman turned occultist Maurice Doreal in 1939? What would you choose to believe?

What about the Istanbul Shem discovered in Turkey? Can you explain to me how we discovered an ancient artifact that looks exactly like a modern astronaut riding a rocket ship and yet is dated to be over 2,500 years old? Whoever created it, did they perhaps only do so because they actually saw such a thing? Did some future race of humans travel back in time to assist the ancients and inspire them to create such an extraordinary object as the Istanbul Shem? Or was this a fabricated object meant to deceive? Does this have anything to do with Project Looking Glass? Is Project Looking Glass really a device discovered from a downed spacecraft that's used to look backward and forward through time? Was it really a chair one could sit in to have their consciousness interfaced directly and used as a sort of steering mechanism? Was it really capable of emitting strong toroidal fields of energy that cycled around a pouch of water at the center that acted as a sort of resonator for instreaming energies from the point of focus held by the operator?

Were scientists really able to collect the data and project it onto video monitors at such high speeds that the images would have to be de-interlaced in order to reveal discernible images? Considering this device was beyond top secret and located in Area 51's S4 level, could it really be true that the project was abandoned because it continued, only giving two possible futures able to gain momentum from a nexus point of December 21, 2012? Didn't the Hopi Indians of

Arizona contain a similar timeline in their ancient writings? If this is true, what were those futures and have we already been given a glimpse as to what those futures were?

If according to whistleblowers, one future was a New World Order and one was a New Golden Age, could Project Looking Glass have been dismantled because since 2012 we have been so deeply entrenched in the positive timeline that the black hats no longer needed it because it just kept revealing over and over again that the White Hats would take control? Or was it confiscated by the white hats in order to thwart certain events such as the public assassination attempt of Donald Trump on July thirteenth of 2024? Is this perhaps why the white hats posted in Q-drop 3555 that "Time travel is fun or…"? Or was there a different reason for that post? How else would you explain Q-drop 2190 that has a picture of Donald Trump fiercely glowing with his fist pumped in the air and the drop says FIGHT, FIGHT, FIGHT and was posted in September of 2018? But if Project Looking Glass wasn't considered time travel because it still didn't allow the user to physically travel through time, then how do you explain all of the similarities and coincidences about Donald Trump and his son Baron in Ingersoll Lockwood's books 'Baron Trump's Marvelous Underground Journey', Travels and Adventures of Little Baron Trump and His Wonderful Dog Bulger' and '1900: Or, The Last President' from the late nineteenth century?

Besides, doesn't the laws of physics tell us that time travel is impossible and wouldn't allow it because if you were to step through a portal where your younger self was located and shot them in the head, then who fired the bullet? But didn't Nikola Tesla secretly invent a form of time travel? And if his invention was confiscated by the black hats to conduct the tragically failed Philadelphia experiment but now the white hats are in control, isn't it possible that the white hats were able to put Nikola Tesla under white hat protection before he could be killed and then have just faked his death? Would you believe me if I said that I've seen evidence of Nikola Tesla giving Donald Trump a great big hug and actually passed away in 2022? Is there something about time travel and portals that simply must remain classified to the very end?

What about Project Stargate? Is it really rumored to be true that the deep state military stayed in Iraq for over ten years after it was liberated? They told us that they were there to liberate the Iraqi people, and if that wasn't believable enough, then we could believe they were there for the oil, but could it really be possible they were actually there for something much more powerful? Why were we never told that in the 1920s a British explorer discovered an ancient Stargate located in the Great Ziggurat that was believed to be the oldest in the world? Was this ancient device really capable of transporting people across interstellar distances in an instant?

And in the 1980s, did Saddam really fortify this ancient complex in old Mesopotamia in order to stop explorers from seeing the incredible secret hidden inside? Was it actually revealed by whistleblowers that ominously strange activity and ancient technology has been seen coming out of the Great Ziggurat? Was it really rumored to be true that some of the activity seen there were ancient beings and technology from our solar system's hidden Planet Nibiru which whips around our sun every 3,600 years? And why is it that whistleblowers about this Stargate or some of the many others around the globe more often than not seem to almost always coincidently go missing?

What else about these Stargates has the cabal been hiding from us? Since we now know for a fact that the black hats used predictive programming in our movies, television, and media in order to normalize nefarious things, as well as allow them to escape the wheels of karma so no one can say they didn't warn us even if we're supposed to believe it's science fiction and couldn't possibly be true, then should we really be surprised to learn that they've also used disclosure films on us as well? If we already know that a disclosure film is when they reveal to us the truth through movies and television, then what are we supposed to think about films like *Jupiter Ascending* or the *Stargate* television series?

Are we really supposed to believe that elements of the *Stargate* television series, such as traveling instantly to other star systems and galaxies through portals as well as sitting in an alien chair to consciously connect to it, are actually original ideas? Is the way the *Jupiter Ascending* film so marvelously depicts Draco reptilians, the

Grays, the immortality substance extracted from humans, as well as how otherworldly people that live for thousands of years in other star systems who actually own planets like Earth really science fiction or even an original idea? Are we really only capable of sending robots to planets like Mars, or is there much more there than they are telling us and certain elites have exclusive access and we're just not invited? Is there something much deeper going on? Or better yet, did the cabal never think "we the people" would awaken to their schemes?

Are we also really supposed to believe that the black hats have never tried to recreate this technology for themselves with massive endeavors like CERN? If we now know for a fact because of thousands of years of ancient wisdom that God is the awareness to all that is and exists within the space between all things including atoms, molecules, and subatomic particles, then should we have ever believed that this particle accelerator or large hadron collider located in Geneva, Switzerland, and affiliated with the UN was ever really looking for the God particle? Do you believe God can be found in a particle?

And why did CERN conduct opening ceremonies right out in the open to the public that when closely examined by someone with knowledge of symbolism seems to be deeply satanic in nature? And how was it that I was able to stumble upon a video online of someone who witnessed and captured actual footage on his cellphone of a satanic ritual of child sacrifice taking place at CERN? So if the UN and CERN are part of the cabal and they had in their possession what appeared to be a highly advanced and very large Stargate, then could the rumors have been true that they were actually trying to open a portal into hell before they were halted by the white hats? Believe whatever you want, it makes you wonder, doesn't it? Am I not merely just asking questions?

> If there's an extraterrestrial event that happens, they'll hoax
> a manmade event piggybacking on an extraterrestrial one.
> Thousands of people will see it. It will simply be a way of them
> testing the system to see what will the people say, what will
> the media say, how are they gonna react? And then all they

would have to do is push a button…*boom*. And the entire event would roll out and everyone on planet earth would be fooled.

—Dr. Stephen Macon Greer, founder of
CSETI and the Disclosure Project

Chapter 6

The Great Reset

The Shot Heard Around the World

The final goal is to eradicate humanity as we know it. Once you understand the final destination, it becomes much easier to look back and identify the psychological conditioning, the biological tampering, the cultural grooming, and the educational prepping that we have been subjected to for decades in preparation to making us accept a post-human future. It takes a lot of physical and psychological abuse to get an intelligent species like ours to agree to its own extinction. Most if not all that has transcended in the last sixty years was designed to get us closer to accepting such a dystopian reality. Whether you care to accept it or not, we live in a hyper-controlled matrix where our perception of reality is meticulously planned, managed, and executed in order to control and steer us in whichever direction they wish. And the direction is a post-human world. For this they first needed to destabilize, dehumanize, and demoralize humanity through every means possible. The destruction of the nuclear family; children being indoctrinated by the state; abortion; the eradication of God and spirituality from education; life in megacities and away from nature, toxic food, air, and water; social media replacing real human connection and interaction; engineered financial crisis and taxation; endless wars and massive migration; stress; anxiety;

depression; drugs and alcohol; constant fear-mongering; moral relativism as the new religion. And I could go on and on about how humanity has been influenced and forced to move away from all the things that give us strength, security, purpose, and meaning. A weak, immoral, disconnected, ignorant, and unhealthy population is an easy target for the next stage. The creation of an entire generation of androgynous beings. Masculinity is under attack, psychologically, culturally, and biologically. Women are being replaced in sports, entertainment, and politics by men pretending to be women. And children are being indoctrinated at school to think that gender is a choice. The transgender movement is not a grassroots movement. It comes from the top. It has nothing to do with people's freedom of expression, sexuality, or civil rights. It's an evil psyop with a clear agenda to get us closer to transhumanism by making us question the most fundamental notion of human identity, our gender. If you don't know who you are, if you already identify as a hybrid between a man and a woman, you will be easily convinced to become a hybrid between human and machine. Gender ideology is the two plus two equals five from George Orwell's *1984* dystopian novel. It's the final test to see whether we will follow the most absurd party line towards our own extinction. But two plus two equals four. And no matter how you choose to dress, call yourself, or change your physique will not change that. The sad reality though is that in the gaslighting process to get us closer to a post-human future, they have mentally and physically harmed an increasing number of children and young people, and it's only getting worse. This must be stopped.
—Laura Aboli, 2023 Better Way Conference

In March of 2020, I was working as an armed guard at a luxurious mom-and-pop watch store in the business district of a real upscale part of town. Just because of the location, our clientele ranged from CEOs who drove super cars who even let me get behind the wheel, to gorgeous models and even professional athletes with photographers following them around. We even had carolers who dressed up like they were from the 1800s dropping in to sing to us around

Christmas. I was also a young, strong, handsome, single guy at the peak of my prowess with the ladies. Living in Trump's America was affordable, abundant, and beyond great. IT WAS THE LIFE. Life was grand. Life was spectacular. And then…the global pandemic hit. "COVID-19," the fake news called it, which I definitely questioned because it was an odd name but also because it was always capitalized. I later came to find out that it was an acronym that stood for (Certificate of Vaccination IDentification-AI).

The AI is because in gematria, the first letter of the alphabet is A and the ninth letter is I. I even saw a video once of a globalist meeting at Davos of this lady talking about COVID-19 so casually and how it was their greatest product to make them even wealthier. I couldn't believe my ears. These people are sick! And then when my research led me to find out that Trump's jabs were only saline and didn't harm anyone but then discovered Biden's batch not only hurt and killed people but also had nanotech in it, I knew that couldn't have been a coincidence. Not to mention that during this tyrannical time in our history, the jab silently, covertly, and ultimately took the lives of over twenty million people worldwide and counting. Which sadly is still the lesser of two evils when you consider that if the sixteen-year plan succeeded, we would be 90 percent extinct. Many were silently killed instantly; many over the course of weeks, some over the course of years from permanently damaged immune systems caused by VAIDS, or Vaccine Acquired Immunodeficiency Syndrome.

However, this wonderful mom-and-pop store I worked at was forced to close their doors, and my security company was forced to relocate me to the coliseum and massive facility next to it where they rounded up all the city's homeless community during the lockdown. I worked with several different law enforcement agencies and security teams there. The pay was good, but the hours were long and stressful, the facility was massive, and the homeless there didn't always behave in a civilized manner. I'll never forget how the bathrooms always smelled like meth and looked like the bathroom straight out of that movie *Saw*. But the one thing that was really suspicious about that situation was that there were well over a thousand homeless people in that facility including the staff and yet none of them had "COVID-

19." And yet the fake news came in to say that everyone had it. This was among one of the first lies by the media I could witness firsthand.

But before I was relocated to the coliseum, I had to work graveyard shift at a haunted hotel that was right by the train station downtown. Considering that it was located in the heart of downtown and was a historic building that was among the first brothels in the old west, it wasn't very hard to believe that it may have been haunted. This place was beyond creepy. The easiest way to describe it would be a smaller version of the mansion from the first *Resident Evil.* Apparently, it was haunted because in the old west, one of the clients at the time was shot in the head with a.357 revolver by his wife who caught him cheating with one of the working ladies at that brothel. They've even had ghost-hunting TV shows that filmed there. And when the world shutdown, I had to work there for at least two weeks before I was relocated to the coliseum.

I didn't believe in all that woo-woo ghost stuff before then, but after having doors slam on me, have the hairs on the back of my neck stand up only on the third floor where the incident happened, and even experienced glasses being moved across the bar and a book flying off the shelf during my shifts, I'm definitely a believer now. Working the graveyard shift there was the creepiest and scariest experience I've ever had. Not only did the back alley look like where young Bruce Wayne's parents were killed in Gotham City, but when you stepped outside, it looked like *Silent Hill,* and there was the eerie feeling of an unknown future because there was absolutely no one in the streets for days on end. Not even wandering vagrants. It was the closest I'd ever felt to encountering the devil in my whole life.

However, during this dark experience, things began to get really weird, and the world started acting in ways it never has before. Tons of things began happening that caused me to start asking questions. Lots of questions. Probably the first question was if I was considered an "essential worker," and if there's this deadly virus out there killing people, are you telling me nobody cares if I die? Then my company gave us an "Essential Personnel Carry Letter" to give to FEMA and the military while the world was locked down. But no FEMA, no military, no tents or hazmat suits anywhere. And I saw the movie

Outbreak, so I had a pretty good idea of what to expect if there was ever a deadly virus unleashed upon the world. Then they told us to just cover your face with either a mask or whatever else you could and you'll be fine. That part was definitely suspicious because unless they were going to start issuing at least gas or oxygen masks, I knew something was up. I already knew that it's very unhealthy to breathe in your own carbon monoxide, but I also knew that a virus is only five nanometers thick and that anything we could put on our faces would be much, much larger. It was like blowing smoke through a chain-link fence.

Then they started saying the only way to protect yourself was to get their vaccine once it was ready in only nine short months. And I already knew it takes a minimum of five-plus years to develop and properly test a vaccine before it's considered safe and effective. So not only that, but politically, what a coincidence that it was an election year and the left along with the fake news have been going way over the top to bash and tear down Donald Trump more than any other political figure in history. Before that, I never cared about politics at all. I had given up on conspiracy theories long after 9/11. And I definitely did not care about military law or constitutional law. But because of the pandemic, now I'm an expert.

The questions I started asking was why did they hate him so much? Who benefits from this? What kind of money is involved when everyone on the planet is mandated to use your product? Why are they trying so hard to convince us to take the jab by offering us a free happy meal or even a free doughnut? And why did all the mom-and-pop stores and restaurants have to close their doors but you were still free to shop at Walmart with a thousand other people as long as you covered your face and joined the rest of the masked crusaders regardless of social distancing guidelines? I even came to find that the word "mandate" originates from Freemasonry and doesn't have anything to do with any real laws.

Definitely one for the record books was that my New Year's resolution for 2020 was to chase more paper, but I never would have dreamed in a thousand years that it would be toilet paper! One thing I found funny at the time was that in Mexico, they didn't stockpile on toilet paper at all like Americans did; they stocked up on beer! I'll never forget how crazy people got over the simplest items. Some places were even selling basic hand sanitizer for up to a hundred dollars. COVID-19 signs and social distancing warnings began popping up everywhere. I even got written up at work because when a coworker would not stop complaining about me not being a hundred feet apart and wearing my face diaper; I absolutely had it that day and gave him the biggest "FU" in front of the rest of the staff that anyone's ever heard.

It was really beginning to feel lonely and isolated being the only one in my world to at least ask questions and not blindly do whatever the media and government told me to do. I ended up losing my job at the coliseum because I was caught not wearing my mask during my lunch break. This is how crazy the world was getting. I also never thought I'd see the day when you were supposed to wear a mask inside a bank and got kicked out for showing your face! Was I the only one who fundamentally knew that the government is supposed to work for us and not tell us what to do? So many things were backward or completely upside down. And as God as my witness, I was determined to find out what the hell was really going on.

This is when I really decided to think for myself and start researching and studying like never before. So I followed the money and started with a few rabbit holes but ultimately ended up doing thousands of hours of research. I always knew in the back of my head all the conspiracies about the New World Order, the Illuminati, and the secret societies. But I never suspected the military would join forces with "we the people" to go to war with them directly and covertly. The black hats even ran a simulation of what a global pandemic would look like and how people would respond, as well as the media, governments, etc., held at a conference called Event 201 suspiciously right before the pandemic even happened. But no matter if they called it the New World Order, Prison Planet, Agenda 21, or the Great Reset, what I discovered they had planned for us truly would have been the end of the world as we know it and would turn out to be the mother of all conspiracies. I saw a video clip that actually showed a really good depiction of what a one-world government would look like, and it was heartbreaking to say the least.

In the video, a woman from one of the major sectors was explaining to another woman who lived in nature what life was like for her. She went on to explain how after the highly significant population reduction, the elite unleashed technologies against us that only supported a post-human future and total control for them. No one was allowed to have family units anymore. Children were no longer had the traditional way. They were all grown in incubators and immediately surrendered to the state. Aside from eliminating the elderly once a certain age was reached, people could not even die properly anymore. Everyone had a kind of chip implant in their heads that would upload their minds to the cloud. So when you die, your mind would just keep going and going trapped to a vessel forever like a complete nightmare. I know it sounds like science fiction, but after connecting all the dots, you'll find out that the cabal has had diabolical plans like this for us for generations. Learning what they wanted to do is definitely a scary thought indeed. But let me share with you some of the ways you've already been fooled and tricked in order to really gain the proper perspective into why there inevitably needed to be a fall to the cabal.

If you take a closer look at the history of some of the words we speak in our daily lives, as well as connect the dots on their origin and hidden meanings that came from the top down, it will blow your mind when you realize that the cabal is not only satanic and Luciferian but has created an entire system for us that was always meant to harm us "useless eaters" by design and indoctrination. Even the word system comes from the Latin word *systema*, which means sewage. Believe it or not, your words are extremely powerful, and the cabal has always known this so they made sure to manipulate English as a way to cast spells on us by having us cast spells on each other.

For instance, SPELLing is SPELL casting. We are BORN into this world. BORN comes from the Old English word *beran*. The word *beran* means unable to bear offspring, unfruitful, bleak, and lifeless. Our children are not even by their definition ours as the word PARENTS is A PAIR who RENTS. Our government, especially our courts, never treated a parent's right to control and direct the upbringing of their child as a fundamental liberty. Look at the word childHOOD. A HOOD is used to cloak and hide. The etymology of the word CHILDREN is *chill* and *dren*. *Chill* means to make cold, and *dren* means a strong and healthy individual. So children are strong and healthy individuals who must be made cold.

In Ballentine's 1948 law dictionary, human being is defined as "see monster" or a human being by birth but in some part resembling a lower animal. In the Oxford New English dictionary of 1901, human is defined as belonging or relative to man as distinguished from God or superhuman beings. The word LIVE spelled backward is EVIL. Our language has been telling us that we are born as monsters who are bleak and lifeless to a pair who rents us from the government and other corporations that indoctrinate us. Our childhood is spent under a cloak because we are evil when we live. Our sentences are made up of WORDS. The Wyrd sisters in Greek mythology are Fates or Witches that control the fates of man. Every word we say directly affects our reality and ultimately our fate. The Egyptian deity Thoth whom we get the word "thought" from and who wrote the *Emerald Tablet* created all pyramids and invented language and writing, intended the original purpose for words to be used for magic. Therefore, could this be more evidence that the mythology behind Thoth the Atlantean is more deception created by the devil?

The words WRITE and RITE are pronounced the same. A rite is a ceremony or ritual. Whenever we are writing with words, we are initiating a ritual. Books contain "chapters." A chapter often refers to a sect of a secret society or religious order. Books also have "pages." To page someone means to summon them. Pages in books made of words are summoning things to enslave or imprison our souls. The word "grammar" comes from the French word *grammaire* or *grimoire*. *Grimoires* were ancient magic books which contained instructions to summon demons. We WAKE up each morning. A wake is a funeral party held for the dead. Each morning we say, "Good morning." Mourning is what you do when you're in deep sorrow and sadness for the loss of a loved one. So we call it a "good mourning" without even realizing it.

We then go to work at our "occupation." When something is occupied, it's like in a "war." We go to war with each other and ourselves when we work at our occupation. An "urn" is for the ashes of the dead. Most people work in the "weekdays." And it's true, you would have to be in a WEAK DAZE to URN a living at your OCCUPATION. During the week, we become weaker and weaker until finally it's the "weekend" and we have become "weakened." Someone who's weakened has no power, which is why many of us turn to alcohol. The word alcohol comes from the word "al-kuhl," which is a body-eating spirit and is also the source of the word "ghoul." We drink "booze" or "boos." Boos are synonymous with spirits that scare you which should be expected when you are drinking "spirits."

It's actually in Hollywood as well. Hollywood is holy wood, which is the wooden staff that sorcerers use to cast spells. We sit down and flip through the channels on television to watch a program, episode, or scene. Funny enough, the original meaning of "episode" is an actual incident or series of unfortunate events. But what's really happening is they are telling us about their vision through "tell-a-vision" and "channeling" a "program" to program us to their will. It's preferable for them that our lives are filled with episodes and scenes in a series of unfortunate events that make our lives difficult and keep us smaller than them. And they haven't just tainted our language and entertainment, but they've also tainted our time as well.

What many people don't know is there's actually supposed to be thirteen months in a year. Each month used to have twenty-eight days. We all commonly know that there are seven days in a week and 365 days in a year. So if there's supposed to be thirteen months, that means each month would have twenty-eight days and each year would have 364 days in a year. And that left one day that was called "the rise of the new sun." But when the cabal changed the Julian calendar to the Gregorian calendar back in 1750, they called it "April Fools' Day" since we were fooled into it. People went unpaid, and there were even protests, which meant people were working thirteen months in the year but only got paid for twelve. The cabal brought in this new Gregorian calendar and removed eleven days out of the year because they understood that history is written by the victors and eventually people would just accept it. We the people are the victors of World War III, which is why I'm writing this book.

The cabal has always been very dark and twisted in their thinking, so they wanted to make sure that newborn babies brought into the world are born in fear. So we've always been told it's nine months to have a baby when in fact it's actually ten months because we're also told forty weeks. So the moment the mother reaches nine months, the baby becomes one week late, two weeks late, three weeks late, and then the mother goes into fear and the baby is born into fear. We even go through this every year when the new year starts in January in the dead of winter when in fact the new year is actually supposed to start in spring when the flowers begin to bloom and Mother Nature begins blossoming with life again. Even the names of the months give us a big clue. But because we rarely ask questions, translate, or decipher language, they've been able to get away with so much even though it's right in our faces. Here's a question…why do several months still have the Latin numbers in their names, such as SEP = 7, OCT = 8, NOV = 9, and DEC = 10? So with that alone, January would be the eleventh month, February the twelfth month, and the new year would begin in March, the way nature intended it.

But it doesn't stop there. Just about every holiday, we've come to know and love has a dark pagan origin, even your birthday. If you've ever had your friends and family sing you the "Happy Birthday" song, you've been tricked into participating in an ancient pagan ritual. We already know that ancient humans used to live for hundreds of years. Even with all our advanced, modern technology, lifespans have still significantly decreased. Legend has it that the "Happy Birthday" song was a curse created by fallen angels. This is why on your birthday, candles are lit, lights are turned off, and everyone gathers in a circle to begin chanting to you like a witch's ritual. This was meant to speed up your aging and seal your fate. So the next time you have a birthday and everyone insists on doing this, go ahead and let them, but just remember that ultimately you have the power and you can refuse to allow a rapid-aging older person to move into your body.

Even Easter and Christmas have absolutely nothing to do with Jesus. In fact, many aspects of traditional Christianity, such as holidays, practices, and doctrines, have nothing to do with Jesus or the Bible. Easter Sunday is actually a Babylonian pagan holiday that celebrates the fertility goddess Ishtar. On the first Sunday after the full moon, they would worship Ishtar by baking cakes, getting drunk, and committing many other unspeakable crimes. Many women were required to lie down at the temple of Ishtar and have sexual relations with anyone who walked in. We paint eggs for Easter because eggs were used as an offering for Ishtar, except instead of being painted with colored paint, these egg offerings would be dipped in the blood of sacrificed infants. And the only reason there are rabbits is because they can bear several litters of young each year due to their very high fertility and only meant it was the perfect symbol for child sacrifice to the goddess Ishtar.

Christmas was also a pagan holiday originally called Saturnalia, which actually predates Christianity itself. It was a weeklong holiday that ran from December 17 through December 25 during Roman times to honor the god Saturn. This weeklong holiday included human sacrifice, intoxication, and naked women caroling and singing in the streets who would then be raped in mass orgies. The only reason we celebrate Christmas on December 25 is because of Emperor Constantine from the fourth century. For a more wholesome alternative, Christians would frequently hold holidays during the same times as pagan festivals.

Christmas fell on the winter solstice; therefore, Emperor Constantine established Christmas on the winter solstice of December 25, AD 336. It's even believed that Jesus's name was actually Yeshua because the letter *J* wasn't even established until long after his time. Many believe his real birthday is actually September 11, which considering what we all know happened in modern times on that day would just be a nice extra middle finger to Christians from the cabal. Christian holidays were meant to replace these evil days of the year, so if you're a Christian, you should still celebrate according to your faith in the church because it's still better than the alternative.

So now that you have a better understanding on how they've programmed us, now allow me to share with you how they have also managed to deprogram us as well. And what I mean by that is how they've hidden the truth about much of our history. As a matter of fact, this is not the first time the cabal has ever attempted a "Great Reset." Believe it or not, they've actually fully succeeded before. We didn't know about it before *because* they succeeded with it. The only reason we know about the Great Reset/NWO/Agenda 21 etc. is because this time they failed.

Have you ever heard of a place called Tartaria? Well, if you haven't, the Tartarian Empire was a technologically advanced civilization that existed long before the 1800s before it was wiped out by a Great Reset, a.k.a. the Mud Flood. Not only was this civilization shown and depicted in old world maps, but it was known to have been a society that developed the ability to harness free energy from the earth's magnetic field and ether. And just with that alone, you can already imagine why they were wiped out. They didn't call a large portion of our history the dark ages because of lost records; they called it that because they never wanted a light to shine on what they've tried to keep hidden.

The photographic and archaeological evidence of the buildings and infrastructure of this lost civilization is astounding. The perfect symmetry, detail, and precision at which these buildings were constructed is absolutely impossible to achieve with mere hammers and chisels. The antennae, gold top, and tesla coil-like pillars of these buildings were highly likely not just for looks. Not to mention the countless photos of old-timey people with electric scooters, devices, and all kinds of other advanced contraptions that should never have existed if we were only supposed to be riding around on a horse and buggy during that time.

Even the document from 1957 containing the directive from the Central Committee of the Communist Party to falsify and rewrite Tartarian history was released on the CIA's website. So be diligent in your research on this one because everywhere you look online, it's referred to as a conspiracy theory. This is why you must ask yourself better questions, such as "Why are they trying so hard to label something as conspiracy theory?" "And if there is a Great Reset attempted to be orchestrated in our lifetime, why is it so hard to believe this could've happened in the past to a society that stepped on the toes of the cabal?" This is why I am not a "conspiracy theorist"; I am a "pattern recognition specialist."

And this brings me to the question, what exactly is "the shot heard around the world"? Well, in the 1760s, when Britain became very greedy and began taxing many things Americans used, such as playing cards, newspapers, glass, lead, and especially tea, this caused the colonists to become very unhappy. On March 5, 1770, the Boston Massacre occurred. Colonists were very upset that British soldiers were on the streets. The massacre ended up killing five colonists and wounded about six. As a result, Britain did end up repealing taxes on every item except for the tea. They didn't want to give up the large tax revenue on something that was deepening their pockets so much.

The colonists did not like this, so they began boycotting the tea that came in from the East India Company and started smuggling Dutch tea. The British parliament passed the Tea Act, which only caused more smuggling and prominent tea smugglers John Hancock and Samuel Adams to protest taxation without representation while still wanting to protect their tea-smuggling operation. This was when a group of colonialist merchants and tradesmen called the "Sons of Liberty" joined up with Hancock and Adams to rally many colonists up to vote against allowing the tea to be unloaded onto their docks.

The governor did not want to go against the British king's demands, so that night, a group from the Sons of Liberty dressed up as Native Americans, snuck onto the ships, and dumped 342 chests of tea into the water. King George the III was not happy, and as a result, he passed the Coercive Acts, which closed the Boston Harbor until the lost tea was paid for. He thought this would halt any kind of a rebellion and stop any remaining colonies from uniting, but it actually caused the exact opposite. All the colonies saw this as evidence of the king's tyranny. On September 5, 1774, the colonists censured

Britain and boycotted all British goods, but this did not cause the king to capitulate.

On April 18, 1775, the king sent a militia over to cease weapons and ammunition from the American colonists. This obviously didn't go over well with the Americans. And when the British reached Lexington early the next morning, there were over seventy colonists waiting. In the silent midst of this confrontation, someone suddenly fired a shot. Nobody knows from which side. However, a brief clash occurred that caused the death of eight Americans. And that was when the American Revolutionary War had officially begun where years later Ralph Waldo Emerson would quote in his 1837 poem "Concorde Hymn" with the words, "By the rude bridge that arched the flood / Their flag to April's breeze unfurled, / Here once the embattled farmer stood / And fired the shot heard around the world."

However, as a pattern recognition specialist, I would be remiss if I did not remind you in how history has a way of repeating itself. This is because the next shot to be heard around the world would spark the official beginning of the second revolutionary war, and this shot took place on January 6, 2021. Except unlike the Sons of Liberty dressing up like Native Americans during the Boston Tea Party, the deep state would hire Antifa along with a myriad of paid actors to masquerade as fake angry Trump supporters, fake medical personnel, and fake cops in what would be the largest false flag psyop ever to be orchestrated and conducted against the American people. I saw the early yet later censored and hidden footage of J6 that was never reported by the fake news. Whether it was the bad acting, countless mistakes, Hollywood stage glass, waistband fake blood pumps and packets, or hundreds of conveniently placed photographers where they didn't belong, there's an inner knowing that real, conservative, God-fearing, America-loving Americans simply don't act the way Antifa was acting that day. January 6 was the fakest thing I've ever seen in my entire life.

When Ashley Babbitt was supposedly shot, it caused shock waves around the world. While in fact, the only real things that happened that day was first, over one million Americans gathered in DC to peacefully protest the stolen election. Second, Donald Trump gave a "Go Home Peacefully" insurrection speech to the people that's required of POTUS to give in that rare circumstance even though the fake news completely ignored it like it never happened. Third, Nancy Pelosi's laptop was covertly confiscated by special forces in the middle of all the Hollywood-style staged mayhem. And last but not least, a small percentage of peacefully protesting honest, innocent Americans were captured by the foreign entity known as Washington, DC, as prisoners of war and stripped of all rights, brutally beaten, and tortured. Absolutely everything else was pre planned, staged, and completely fake. This is including the J6 shot heard around the world. What does that tell you about how far the black hats were willing to go?

Not only did they completely fabricate stories from scratch, but they also completely hid and ignored anything that goes against their masters. These people are sick! In case you haven't noticed by now, the subtitles for all my chapters are infamous drops that only true fellow patriots and digital soldiers would understand. So considering what the fake shot heard around the world was, what was the real shot heard around the world? Some might say it was the assassination attempt on Trump in the summer of 2024. I would say that it was the "jab" and how following it were millions of people dying suddenly and silently all over the world in the weeks and months to come. And although the shot itself and millions of people crying aloud with their voices silenced and censored all over social media was not heard, what was heard around the world was the stream of never-ending media lies and them still pushing the jab even though countless people were dropping dead all over the globe. And because their false flag psyop was still effective on a large part of the populous, well, over half of all Americans were labeled domestic terrorists overnight.

So what did the secret families and globalists have planned for us before their plans were thwarted by the white hats? Well, they wanted a one-world government; one-world cashless currency; one-world central bank; one-world military; an end to all national sovereignty; an end to all privately owned property ("You'll own nothing and be happy," they would say); an end to all family units; depopulation and control of all population growth and density; mandatory multiple vaccines; universal basic income (austerity); a microchipped society for purchasing, travel, tracking, and controlling; implementation of a world Social Credit System (like China); all appliances hooked into the 5G monitoring system (Internet of things); government-raised children; government owned and controlled schools, colleges, and universities; an end to private transportation, such as owning cars, all businesses owned by government, and a few corporations; a restriction to all nonessential air travel; all humans concentrated into human settlement zones; no more irrigation; no more private farms and grazing livestock; no more privately owned land; a ban of all natural cures and remedies; and last but not least, an end of all fossil fuels.

There was also the silent shot not heard around the world thanks to President Trump, especially for all those who hated him. President Trump tweeted the phrase "COVFEFE" and was relentlessly mocked by the fake news because they thought he spelled the word coffee wrong. Whereas "COVFEFE" was code for being a part of the periodic table of elements comprised of cobalt and two molecules of iron which helped create the magnetic field that protected millions from the 5G frequency energy weapon of mass destruction known as COVID-19. When set to 60 gigahertz, oxygen molecules in the atmosphere interact with radio frequency signals and begin causing significant attenuations and vibrations. At 60 gigahertz oxygen gets absorbed and the interference within our own lungs results in severe pneumonia and flu-like symptoms. C-19 was a gain of function weapon developed by Dr. Anthony Fauci with the financial support of the NIH helping move his bio labs to Sudan, Ukraine and Taiwan and was considered the gun. The 5G Huawei telecommunications equipment was the bullet.

Thanks to Trump's quick and decisive action, he saved more than half of the U.S. population and stopped that deadly shot from ever being heard around the world. Whereas I smirk whenever I meet someone who hates him because not only do they often not even know why, but because they haven't the slightest clue how President Trump saved them from hell, and they don't even know it. And what would throw many sleepers and black-pilled patriots off is that the White Hats would allow the Black Hats to believe they could introduce certain draconian laws such as central bank digital currency, social credit scores, assault weapons bans and even election interference without repercussions. They allowed this to happen to make the Black Hats reveal their true intentions, while waking up the people and simultaneously arresting political figures for treason in the background. All while knowing the fake news would never report it. Don't forget that the white hats always needed to deceive the black hats to lead them where they wanted them while simultaneously ensuring victory in Trump's secret war against THE STATE OF ISRAEL. Hence the Q posts that mention Israel being saved for last.

This is what they actually had planned for us. A Great Reset. But thanks to Donald Trump and the white hats, we only got to experience a greatly shortened and highly sped-up version of this plan so that the disoriented and sped-up effects of such a chaotic plan would not go smoothly and only cause the people to notice something wrong and begin slowly and organically waking up to become God's army against the devil. This Great Reset would ultimately transition into instead what is now known as the "The Great Awakening."

Allowing for the book, after all, being a parody, something like *1984* could actually happen. This is the direction the world is going in at the present time. In our world, there will be no emotions except fear, rage, triumph, and self-abasement. The sex instinct will be eradicated. We shall abolish the orgasm. There will be no loyalty, except loyalty to the party. But always there will be the intoxication of power. Always at every moment, there will be the thrill of victory, the sensation of trampling on an enemy who is helpless. If you want a picture of the future, imagine a boot stamping on a human face forever. The moral to be drawn from this dangerous nightmare situation is a simple one, don't let it happen. It depends on you.

—Eric Arthur Blair, a.k.a. George Orwell

Chapter 7

⁓◈⁓

The Great Awakening

Nothing Can Stop What Is Coming. Nothing.

God doesn't give the hardest battles to his toughest soldiers; He creates the toughest soldiers through life's hardest battles.

—Unknown

I'll never forget the summer of 2021. I was working security at an intelligence agency in the inner city of downtown where the high rises towered over and encompassed you in a deep urban environment. The Biden regime had officially taken over the presidency of the now bankrupt corporation of USA Inc. It was my first year ever of experiencing a communist America, and I had already been in countless confrontations in my daily life with people at every public place I used to frequent because I absolutely refused to wear a mask or show my papers. Even my company tried to mandate that experimental jab. So I gave them the finger and told them they could get rid of me if they didn't like it. Good thing they still needed me.

One night when it was cold, wet, and raining, I was patrolling the property and noticed on our cameras that a homeless man was curled up in a fetal position on our smoking area bench in the alley between buildings with no clothes except for some underwear. He was absolutely freezing and soaked. Naturally, I came to his rescue and gave him my expensive work jacket. I wasn't supposed to give away company property or be outside in the soaking rain without a jacket, but I didn't care. He needed my help, and I was determined to help him in any way that I could, come hell or high water! But if I would've known the events that were to follow afterward, I would have at least tried to figure out a different way. I ended up catching pneumonia and was forced to go to the one place that actually felt comparable to being on the trains to the Auschwitz's concentration camp in the Nazi, Germany, era…the hospital.

I knew I had pneumonia, and after everything I learned about what was really going on, I knew it was going to be an uphill battle. I tried every kind of medicine and treatment I could, but nothing worked. I even tried homemade hydroxychloroquine, but I was already too far along. I wanted ivermectin, but it was almost impossible to find at that time. I couldn't breathe, and I was completely out of options. I also knew exactly what the hospital would do, especially after it was becoming common knowledge that even if you go to the hospital with a gunshot wound or if you got into a motorcycle accident, you've got "COVID-19." So left with no other options, I called the ambulance to come and get me.

Once they came, the first thing they did was put me on oxygen. And as soon as they did, I was cured, and I felt great! I no longer saw any reason for me to even go the hospital anymore. But they didn't let me. When I got to the hospital, they rolled me into a room where they gave me some unknown meds and told me they were going to test me for COVID-19. Because I had previously learned that the PCR (polymerase chain reaction) test not only contained carcinogenic ethylene oxide (a cancer-causing agent) but was also rigged so that every thirty-four out of thirty-five tests were preassembled to be false positives, I told the lady they better not even think about shoving that cancer stick up my nose. But when I wasn't looking, she actually had the gull to sneak it up my nostril without my permission. I told her I was going to sue her, but she didn't even care and just left never to be seen again.

I was there for three long days because they said I not only had pneumonia, but I apparently had "COVID-19 pneumonia." I never heard of anything so ridiculous in my entire life. And I told the doctor upfront that I was not going to take the jab under any circumstances. But since they said I had COVID-19, they had to at least pump me up with Dr. Fauci's primary recommended treatment for COVID-19 besides the jab…a failed drug from the 1980s that did absolutely nothing against COVID-19 that was called remdesivir. The only thing remdesivir did was cause organ failure and death. I had no idea what it was at the time, but later I learned that only 30 percent of people who have taken it actually survived.

When I was finally being released from the hospital, they actually told me that my PCR test came back negative. I was furious, and I still had to be on oxygen at home for at least another week. However, the pain in my internal organs and bathroom trouble lasted for three whole months because of the remdesivir. I never took any legal action since I didn't really feel empowered to do so in a communist country where our legal system has been weaponized against us. So at the very least, when I received the bill, I tore it up and threw it in the trash. I was just thankful to have survived the trains.

Lots of strange global events began happening between 2020 and beyond that were confusing to many but intriguing to digital soldiers, patriots, and pattern recognition specialists like me. The white hats really started cleaning up house behind the scenes, and it was only if you knew the government is our employees, you could see past the fake news and had alternative sources of information and history that you could connect the dots and see what was really going on. And the white hats definitely did not make it easy. It was really, really hard decoding Q-drops, collaborating with fellow patriots, and organically forming a grassroots movement that went against everything the mass-brainwashed populous was programmed to believe. All I can say is that MKUltra is a "bitch!" In the beginning, my own family and friends wouldn't hear a thing I said because they had been programmed their entire lives. I still remain the only one in my immediate family that's never been jabbed.

But as time went on, as the white hats continued the greatest show on earth, more and more people began slowly waking up until eventually the day would come when the people would begin to realize that it was time to stop waiting for "something to happen" and realize that lots of stuff has been happening the entire time, but you had to look for it and find the right sources because the media didn't report any good guy progress because they still worked for the bad guys. The white hats did their part by conducting mass arrests on over five hundred thousand sealed indictments behind the scenes and opening up our republic for us to take back. It eventually became our job as a people to take our republic back ourselves because as much as I hate to say it, we didn't win the first revolutionary war like they've had us believe all this time. It has finally come our time to finish what our ancestors and forefathers had started. So while we've been waiting on the military, they've been waiting on us. They've done their part, and it was a lot. More than you can imagine. The rest was up to us.

But that would first come at a heavy cost of the silent jab taking effect while at the very same time the world was under heavy psyop and experiencing mass formation psychosis for the first time. Imagine a war in which the majority of one side didn't know they were at war, ridiculed those that did, and were blindly obedient to their enemy. What the media was putting out there and what fellow patriots were seeing was completely different. For instance, when the masses saw fences going up around the White House to keep "domestic terrorists" out, fellow patriots knew that the white hats put up those fences to keep the black hats along with special operations inside considering that the barbed wire was facing inward.

The white hats had turned the White House into a courthouse to hold military tribunals for all the guilty parties. This was first disclosed by an insider that went by the name of Juan O' Savin who predicted what the fences would be used for long before anyone else. There were even photos and videos from fellow patriots, such as "Richard Citizen Journalist" who lived in DC that were able to show us evidence that tribunals were being held, DUMBs were being flooded, and children were being rescued all while the media was only reporting a fence being used to keep "Trump supporters" out. I remember seeing loads of federal buildings being closed and surrounded by sandbags as well as storm drains having water flow out of them as if something was definitely going on underground.

Then there were global incidents, such as the massive *Evergreen* ship that blocked the Suez Canal. "Evergreen" was Killary's code name by the way. People thought that was just an accident while truthers, Anons, and patriots followed what really unfolded behind the scenes. The white hats definitely had a sense of humor because when space force and the Alliance remotely took control of that ship, satellite images revealed how the ship was steered in such a direction to form the shape of a very specific male appendage or perhaps a middle finger depending on how your imagination wanted to see it in order to mock the cabal and give a hat tip to patriots and Anons.

What the media never would have revealed about that incident in a million years was that secret US and Russian special forces all part of the Alliance took control of that ship and ended up finding six stories of shipping containers of guns, bombs, missiles, and weapons of mass destruction, over thirty years' worth of climate change DEWs, a nuclear warhead heading to Romania, over two million vials of deadly vaccines, and over 1,350 dead children all while the ship was rigged with explosives. Thankfully, over 1,200 kids who were still alive were rescued after the explosives were disarmed.

And that's just the tip of the iceberg when it comes to what the white hat military went through behind the scenes in order to secretly save the world. There have already been reports of soldiers being severely traumatized from some of the evil they had to endure. Having to fight battles underground where they witnessed children locked in cages and being experimented on and even top-secret alien stuff we were never supposed to know about. The Alliance of militaries all around the world worked in unison to clear out everything these sick pedos have built. There were unbelievably massive underground trafficking tunnels and DUMBs globally in places, such as Antarctica, South Africa, China, Taiwan, Ukraine, Europe, North and South America, Hollywood, and even Disney World.

Hollywood was a ghost town for a period of time. Only Apple, Amazon, Netflix, and a few other major studios were still cutting checks. Many of the other organizations were being cleaned out of pedos. Even in Disney World, a sheriff gave a press conference speech about how they successfully completed a sting operation where they busted hundreds of employees for everything from pornography, molestation, grooming, and even the rape of children. This ranged from hotel concierges all the way up to previous CEOs and vice presidents. Since Disney was established with the help of the CIA, Walt Disney was a thirty-third-degree Freemason, and the park was considered its own sovereign nation of pedos with its own money. Is it really that hard to believe that Disney has been an MKUltra project since its inception, especially with all the subliminal stuff most people already know they've been caught putting in their movies and shows? These people are sick!

And then there were some of the infamous but secret gun battles that took place between the white hats and black hats behind the scenes that actually got leaked out. This governmental civil war contained such firefights between special forces and FBI in the DC FBI building, with Delta Forces seizing thousands of firearms on an eighteen-wheeler being shipped to IRS agents in DC and even the marines trying to stop treasury agents from printing more fake currency at the Federal Reserve. Unfortunately, four marines were killed in that one and were forced to retreat from being outnumbered. U.S. Special Forces even rescued 27 innocent J6ers from a Deep State prison in the Aleutian Islands whose only crime was peacefully visiting the capitol building on January 6th. These prisoners had no trials, were tortured beyond belief and one of the females was even raped repeatedly by the guards. How these innocent patriots were treated from the beginning was not only unconstitutional, but against the Geneva Convention and inhumane. All DHS Guards on the island were shown no mercy and dealt with swiftly either by sniper headshots or slit throats. Another victory was a battle between U.S. Marines and FEMA agents in Tornado Alley where 31 agents were swiftly eradicated from the earth without mercy for planning to terrorize citizens whose towns were flattened by artificial F3 and F4 tornadoes. Instead of coming to the aide of citizens who just experienced absolute catastrophe with food, water and shelter, FEMA was instead planning to terrorize these American patriots with what was found in their possession to be a cache of 300 rifles and 165 handguns with stockpiles of ammunition all confiscated by the Marines.

This is how sick the Black Hats were and the kind of madness that went on silently in our own backyards while America was still sleepwalking. There was even one tragic incident where over two hundred white hat soldiers of the Alliance were killed in a trap set by the cabal. This was reported by an amazing, God-fearing retired navy patriot who went by the name of "Gene Decode." This is all just a small portion of the big picture of what the white hats sacrificed for us in this battle for planet earth. Since no one else is going to remember these silent knights, the least I can do is share with the world the sacrifice they made in this book.

But whether it was purposely not reported by the fake news like the people arresting the military in Kazakhstan or out there for everyone to see like the ridiculous Chinese spy balloon, the revolution was not televised and the show carried on. No matter if it was political—such as cocaine being found at Biden's house, a dead body being found at Obama's house, a male prostitute being found at Pelosi's house, an illegal server being found at Clinton's house—they still sent the FBI to raid Donald Trump's house for declassified documents that could expose them. If it was sci-fi in nature where the news was bombarding us with distractions about aliens, the revolution was not televised and the show carried on.

Whether it was a false flag, such as the FBI attempting to dress up as terrible imitations of Trump supporters marching down the street to try to make us look bad, or whether it was a distraction, such as train derailments or bridge bombings to steal our attention away from more elitist pedo exposure, the revolution was not televised and the show carried on. Even when many police officers in Australia and New Zealand abused their authority by strangling, beating, and stomping on the faces of the unmasked and unvaccinated protesters and forced them into quarantine camps to be abused even more or when the unvaccinated were force-vaccinated by authorities in Brazil, the revolution was not televised and the show carried on.

Whether it was the truckers being the tip of the spear and putting a stop to all shipments in Ottawa, Canada, or the students walking out of classes at Oakdale High School in California refusing to comply with forced mask mandates, the revolution was not televised and the show carried on. It didn't matter if native tribal locals in Wellington, New Zealand, gathered by the tens of thousands at their government buildings to conduct tribal dances and pierce the skies with their chants and war cries or if hundreds of police surrounded the Bayside Mall in Miami, Florida, because of aliens coming out of a portal from Antarctica even though we were told police were there because of a few kids fighting with sticks, the revolution was not televised and the show carried on.

Even when the Mama Bears were labeled as domestic terrorists because they went to their local school board meetings to fight against their children being forced to participate in "Drag Time Story Hour" while having pedo porn and grooming books in their libraries or when children spoke up at these same meetings to have their voices heard about men being allowed in women's sports and women's restrooms while also having critical race theory being taught in order to indoctrinate our children to become divided by race, the revolution was not televised and the show carried on. Whether it was Trump's Underground social media accounts that revealed his plans to destroy the Deep State as well as his Trump Card and underground campaigning or if it was all of the Deep State's attempts to attack, indite, convict, arrest and even assassinate him when he became bait to expose the three branches of government such as executive, administrative and judicial, the revolution was not televised and the show carried on.

Even if it was the secret debut of the gray hats creating an illusion of good vs. evil or the compartmentalized group of scientists, contractors and engineers who called themselves the Green Hats who were tricked by the Cabal to create various technologies they thought would be used for good, or of the red hats; a group of ex-military civilians whose hearts were noble but whose intentions were bloody and didn't agree with the white hats allowing the election to be stolen because although their frustration was shared by many patriots and libertarians, their intentions were understood if they really caused earthquakes on the eastern seaboard to attack the deep state directly. However, those same intentions may not have grasped the magnitude of this war and the importance of luring the deep state out with a military sting operation in order to ensure this never happens again. Because if the people recognize the enemy, then the enemy will never be able to resurface. Not to mention that if you merely execute these evil ones without trial and due process and not in defense but only in offense, then it does not honor God or help our ascension and you yourself inherently become the Cabal. I fully understand that on the surface this war needed to be fought according to the law and by the book and that behind the scenes this war was being fought kinetically with no Geneva Convention or constitution and strictly by any means necessary for the sake of saving humanity no matter what it takes. I completely understand the motive of the Red Hats, especially since it has the Black Hats looking over both shoulders. I'm merely saying we should do our best in honoring what we know in our hearts God would want us to do to further the goal of peace and prosperity. Whether these disruptions were legitimate or another psyop, what I do know for sure is that the revolution was not televised and the show carried on.

Whether it was a deep freeze in Texas, snow in Brazil, typhoons in Shanghai, hurricanes in Michoacan, floods in Vietnam, tornadoes in Wuhan, fires in Maui, earthquakes in Turkey and the US eastern seaboard, as well as the three Gorges Dam collapsing in China or biblical solar eclipses, planet Nibiru entering our solar system, and even a two-thousand-year-old Bible prophesied geyser of water bursting out of a rock in the ground of the Negev Desert that created a river for the locals, the revolution was not televised and the show carried on. Even when big tech censored anti-vaxxers, election deniers, and the cures for cancer or when MKUltra started Project Blue Bird that became Twitter was hijacked by the white hats so the Twitter files could be unleashed to then become the X files, the revolution was not televised and the show carried on.

It didn't matter if it was constant nuclear scares of World War III coming because of this country versus that country or when awakened patriots began migrating to alternative free speech platforms to create podcasts, music, and entertainment to wake up the sleepers, the revolution was not televised and the show carried on. Whether it was "Trans" mass shooters scaring us into giving up our

Second Amendment rights or if it was US State Nationals serving council members by putting them on notice about abusing our children in schools in Maricopa County that eventually led to all ridiculous mask and vax mandates being lifted everywhere, the revolution was not televised and the show carried on.

Whether it was a ridiculously black hat, staged false flag with hired crisis actors or central casting such as the 'January 6th Insurrection' or even when prices began to soar for everything that destroyed our economy and illegal migrants continuing to flood in through our border from all over the world regardless of background and criminal history, as well as the cartels taking over US territory, the revolution was not televised and the show carried on. This sped-up version of the sixteen-year plan in order to prevent civil war felt like an eternity for awakened, battle-fatigued, unplugged patriots who have been awake since the beginning. Many people will never know just how hard it was to keep quiet and hold our tongues for years, knowing what was really happening in a world where the average person as well as our loved ones were so hopelessly dependent on the system that they would fight to the death to defend that system. Even when the white hats finally had the scale of awakened and asleep tipped in their favor, they always knew that some people would simply never wake up.

Even when an awakened patriot would divulge the truth to a sleeping loved one, that individual would often refuse to accept whatever truth was given because their ego would never allow them to believe that they've been conned their wholes lives and their reality was fabricated and not organic. As Samuel Clemens (a.k.a. Mark Twain) once so eloquently put it, "It is far easier to convince someone of a lie than it is to convince them that they've already been fooled." For years, many patriots felt so isolated and alone that sometimes the only place to find refuge and sanity was in the seeking out and company of other patriots who could be confided in.

Some anons would even have one or two episodes of their podcasts where they would get highly emotional in tears or fly off the handle from feeling so isolated, alone and hopelessly misunderstood. I share this struggle and will never forget how bad it felt. As the world began slowly waking up one person at a time and events began unfolding first as drips until ultimately into a flood during the storm, when Q said that nothing could stop what was coming, it's because they understood that life is more powerful than death and that if they could plant the seed of faith and patriotism in the people to organically fight to take their sovereignty back from the evil tyrants like how this great nation was started, then absolutely nothing would be able to stop what was coming. The white hats would destroy the deep state roots in the background by systematically and sequentially crashing Deep State systems in a planned manner and not all at once in order to prevent Civil War and panic among the people while it was up to the people to work together in cutting down the deep state tree of remaining evil minions.

Slowly but surely, the people first needed to gradually wake up and identify how we were all being enslaved before we could finally be truly free from the evil grip of the cabal, such as recognizing that we've only been operating in the lowest form of law which is maritime, admiralty, and corporate law and needed to begin operating in common, trust, and nature's law once again. We the people needed to learn how to stand in honor as a living man or woman and reclaim our status as the body sovereign and begin thinking like creditors and no longer like debtors by creating social compacts and trusts by hiring trustees to uphold them based on free will. Recognizing that we the people put all the money into the banks and create all the world's wealth and the fact that the banks can't survive without us. To redirect attention on them and ask for their credentials instead of allowing them victory by assumption of our ignorance.

We needed to remember to declare ourselves as kings and queens and start acting like it by setting intention and making spiritual, personal, family, and community declarations and protecting our kingdoms as a top priority if we were to restore the world's republics from de facto to de jure. We needed to recognize things, such as the simple difference between John Smith and JOHN SMITH and how they created a Cuesta Que Vie Trust and a corporation in our names at birth. We needed to recognize how our marriage certificates gave them our property and our children, as well as how our driver's licenses and registration gave them our vehicles. We needed to recognize how all cities, counties, and states are foreign corporations with a zip code overlay that enabled our mortgages to be funded by us but yet our homes and land would still be claimed by the state.

We needed to learn how they controlled the sheriffs, police, jails, schools, and municipalities by the fact that the 670 courthouses in the US were also administrative banks (a.k.a. money changers). But we also needed to recognize that 99 percent of the devil's army has no idea who they really work for; hence, the greatest lie of convincing people of his nonexistence. We also needed to learn how all fraud vitiates fraud, global elite pull all strings, their system requires our ignorance, and that this war was not only of good vs. evil but also awake vs. asleep. We also needed to learn how the pen truly is mightier than the sword by learning how to stand up to our employees by first serving them a notice of liability and grant them an opportunity to cure, then by providing them a writ of quo warranto, which was then followed by a waiver of tort and then providing them default judgment, council of twelve signatures, and ultimately inform them of a notice to the military to conduct tribunals on treasonous leaders. But most important of all, we needed to realize the power of just saying no.

But as I close out the "greatest story never told" about the war to end all wars regardless of whatever happens to me or how my life unfolds, I am only reminded that my only purpose for writing this book was to serve God and humanity with the very best I could while alive. Knowing firsthand how much of a nightmare it has been walking through the valley of the shadow of death, I only wanted to leave our children and future generations with a solid history book of what really happened from someone born of this "legendary generation." To once again quote Mark Twain, "The two most important days of your life are the day you were born and the day you find out why." This is why I can gladly say how blessed and fortunate I am to have done my part in this war of good vs. evil and can die happy no matter what the result or effect I had on the world was. But to anyone who may think that everything in this book is lies, false, or complete garbage, then by all means continue on living your life believing whatever you choose. That's none of my business. Even if hypothetically I'm completely wrong about everything, I'm still better off spending my time shining my light of hope and faith then being right at the end and getting to say, "See, I told you we were all screwed!" But when it comes to all the information in this book, I only ask you to use your imagination and ask yourself one question if you believe this book is false, "What if it's not?"

My final message to the brave men and women in our militaries around the world who took part as white hats in this great war: "Thank you for your unimaginable service and unimaginable sacrifice in saving the world from total annihilation." My final message to the black hats in the cabal: "We the people and our children are NOT for sale." As for my final message to the pure-blooded patriots who fought for humanity's transition into a new quantum financial system, the Age of Aquarius, a New Golden Age, and a New Earth that the meek inherit, I leave you with a quote I found by an unknown patriot:

> Message to the unvaccinated: "Even if I were pollinated and fully vaccinated, I would admire the unvaccinated for withstanding the greatest pressure I have ever seen, even from partners, parents, children, friends, colleagues, and doctors. People who were capable of such personality, courage, and critical ability are undoubtedly the best of humanity. They are everywhere, in all ages, levels of education, states, and ideas. They are of a special kind; they are the soldiers that every army of light wants to have in its ranks. They are the parents that every child wants to have and the children that every parent dreams of having. They are beings above the average of their societies; they are the essence of the people who have built all cultures and conquered horizons. They are there, next to you, they look normal, but they are superheroes. They did what

others could not; they were the tree that withstood the hurricane of insults, discrimination, and social exclusion. And they did it because they thought they were alone and believed they were the only ones. Banned from their families' tables at Christmas, they never saw anything so cruel. They lost their jobs, let their careers sink, had no more money, but they didn't care. They suffered immeasurable discrimination, denunciation, betrayal, and humiliation, but they kept going. Never before in humanity has there been such a "casting." Now we know who are the best on planet Earth: women, men, old, young, rich, poor of all races or religions, the unvaccinated, the chosen of the invisible ark, the only ones who managed to resist when everything collapsed. That's you, you passed an unimaginable test that many of the toughest marines, commandos, Green Berets, astronauts, and geniuses could not withstand. You are made of the stuff of the greatest who ever lived, those heroes born among ordinary men who glow in the dark."

—Unknown

Acknowledgments

When our grandchildren ask us what we did during the last great war and how we stood up, these are a few of the Anons, patriots, and digital soldiers who fought the deep state cabal head-on, bravely, and tirelessly to inspire this book. All of whom each did their part in history to help save the world and ensure a bright future for humanity's children for many generations to come.

A very special thanks to Donald John Trump, Kash Patel, Dan Scavino, Michael Flynn, Gene Ho, Scott McKay the patriot street fighter of Revolution Radio, retired Navy veteran Gene Decode, Cirsten Weldon (RIP), Melissa Redpill of Freedom Force Battalion, Nicholas Veniamin from NVTV, Dave from X22 Report, LT from And We Know, Marine verteran Sarge from ICONS, Mary and commander Thor from We the People News, Kerry Cassidy from Project Camelot, Patriot from Patriot Underground, Michael Baxter from Real Raw News, Charlie Ward, Jason Q, Ethan Lucas, Mil Spec Ops Monkey from Monkey Werx, Navy Seal veteran Michael Jaco, Michelle Fielding, Derek Johnson, David Wilcock of Divine Cosmos, Billy Carson from 4BK, David Nino Rodriguez from Nino's Corner, SG Anon from Q News Patriot, Christian Patriot News, Santa Surfing from Beach Broadcast, Dylan Monroe (the Map Maker), Whiplash 347, Q the Storm Rider, Pepe Lives Matter, Il Donaldo Trumpo, Tippy Top Patriot," Richard Citizen Journalist, Top G Andrew Tate, Myron Gaines and Walter Weekes (Fresh Prince CEO) from Fresh & Fit, Stew Peters, Juan O' Savin (JFK Jr.?), William Thompkins, Jordan Maxwell, David Straight, Michelle (Miki) Klann from Our Great Awakening, James O'Keefe from project Veritas, Lara Logan, Kari Lake, Rosanne Barr, Kevin Sorbo, Jim Breuer, Hi-Rez, Pryme Minister, Dr. Jan Halper Hayes,

Dr. Steven Macon Greer, Dr. Richard Walford, Julie Ann Hanson-Luckett MS, Army Specialist OIF Veteran Paul Sanders Bothel, and Marine Staff Sergeant OEF Veteran David Mikael Perez McGraw and Chuck Wilkins.

I also give great thanks to Carlos, Tony, Angel, Jeremy, Sal, Lucas, Kevin, Joseph, Andrew (RIP) and Daniel for challenging my beliefs so hard that it caused me to push through harder and strengthen my beliefs into a convicted knowing.

Another very special thanks to a few fans who supported and believed in me throughout this entire journey. You know who you are. Adriana and Benjamin Ramos, Kimberly Delia Figueroa, Alegra Herring, Caroline Rodriguez, Christina Aguilar, Christine Thurstone, Donfred Metayer, Kyle and Megan, Lenayya Baker, Lori, Elle, Isaiah, Kayji and Maribelle Morales, Matt Burke, Michele Lee Backer, my neighbors Cassandra and Tina, Richard L. Myers (Manatee in the Mirror), Teresa Lopez, Tiffany D. Randon, Caitlyn Brown, Todd Holten, and to Odon Rodriguez Siles (RIP) for giving me my dearest beloved wife Lucia and my new family. Thank you all for believing in me so that I could carry on and push forward to do my part in this historic battle between good and evil. I will carry you all in my thoughts and heart until our paths cross again in this world or the next.

About the Author

J. L. Morales desired the wisdom of the ages more than anything else. And because of that, he was put on a very difficult path in order to obtain it. As a young boy, he was always up to no good, fighting, experimenting with drugs, skipping class, and dropping out of high school; he was only familiar with a life of crime. He first became humbled when a few of his so-called friends left him for dead on the street with alcohol poisoning. When the judge gave him a second chance, he decided not to waste it, turn his life around, and begin giving back. When his brother suggested breakdancing, he saw this as an opportunity to become more than he was. Through that, he found the inspiration to go back to school and become the first college grad in his family. After working everything—from door-to-door sales, cleaning toilets, construction, to driving a truck across the country as a welder—he finally found true fulfillment as a security guard in Denver. Working with the homeless and putting his life on the line to serve his community in some of the most dangerous areas of town taught him to truly live each day as his last. Only by earning his stripes on the street has he found the desire to begin writing and help those beyond his local community for the rest of his life. As a loving son, brother, stepfather, husband, and native Coloradan, he still resides in the Centennial State.